Advance Praise for *Do Not Di*

"*Do Not Disclose* is hard to put down, a haunting, poetic journey, the search for lost childhood, like a letter from someone we did not want to see anymore, nor want to open for the fear of finding inside it—a truth."

—**John Bernstein**, prize-winning screenwriter, playwright, and Professor of Holocaust in Film and Israeli Cinema at the Elie Wiesel Center for Jewish Studies

"Krygier is an exquisite writer and *Do Not Disclose* is her masterpiece. In lyrical prose, she recounts the bittersweet journey of excavating the truth in her own family and that of a complete stranger. When astonishing twists and turns lead her on a path she never expected to travel, she stays the course with courage and commitment and ultimately finds her way home."

— **Linda Schreyer**, award-winning screenwriter and author of *Tears and Tequila*

"A remarkable personal journey and deeply moving tale of family secrets. A must-read."

— **Eva Nagorski**, award-winning screenwriter, director, and author of *The Down and Dirty Dish on Revenge*

"The postcard protagonist in Leora Krygier's exquisite memoir proves that time is no impediment to love."

—**Carolyn Howard Johnson**, multi award winning author and poet.

Praise for *Keep Her*:

"Krygier's vivid, immersive prose . . . a recommended read for creative romantics everywhere."

— *School Library Journal*

"*Keep Her* will engage fans of contemporary fiction. Fans of meant-to-be romance stories will not be disappointed."

—Voya Magazine

"Krygier writes like she knows the characters personally. I have never read a story as filled with passion and regret as this book."

—TeenReads

"This vibrantly dazzling literary cocktail on the restorative powers of love will leave reader's hearts renewed."

—Popsugar

"Discussing topics such as environmental protection and adoption, *Keep Her* is a refreshingly honest read."

—BuzzFeed

DO NOT DISCLOSE

DO NOT DISCLOSE

A Memoir of Family Secrets Lost and Found

Leora Krygier

Published 2021
Printed in the United States of America
Print ISBN: 978-1-64742-159-5
E-ISBN: 978-1-64742-160-1
Library of Congress Control Number: 2021906589

For information, address:
She Writes Press
1569 Solano Ave #546
Berkeley, CA 94707

She Writes Press is a division of SparkPoint Studio, LLC.

For Noam, Liv, and Ella

One

My head started to throb when I saw the words, underlined, on the small, torn-off note: _Do Not Share This_.

It should have been just a quick drop-off of some insurance forms at my parents' house, and I was just about to leave when I noticed it—a small note poking out of a slim file on their foyer floor. It was halfway out of a file, barely noticeable among the papers and boxes that were strewn all over their normally pristine living room and entranceway, the unusual chaos part of my mother's monthlong clean-up-and-throw-away campaign. I bent down a little to get a closer look. The handwriting on the note itself was unfamiliar, but the name on the file, in my father's unmistakable handwriting—_Rhea_—wasn't, and together the note and the name pushed the replay button in my head, a rerun of that night ten years ago, the night of the phone call, the night when all hell broke loose.

"You can't even stay for a cup of coffee?" my mother asked. She looked pretty today in the blouse I'd given her a year ago for her birthday but that she'd never worn till now.

I snapped back up. "I can't. I have to go. Sorry. I really have to go. I'm already late for court," I said, and took a couple of steps toward the door.

"You're wearing jeans to court?"

I stopped. "Don't worry. No one can see what I'm wearing underneath the black robe." Wearing jeans under my robe had now become

1

part of my mini-rebellion against the stiff suits and bow ties I'd been expected to wear in my earlier years as a new lawyer.

"Ah," she said with a shrug. "Well, then," she began, and I started toward the door again. "You should be happy," my mother suddenly chirped.

I stopped again. "Happy?"

"Yes, happy I'm sparing you."

"Sparing me?"

"Yes. Sparing you having to throw away our junk after we're gone," she announced, as though she'd bought me an expensive gift. "Your father . . . ," she said, and then shook her head. "He won't throw anything away."

I looked down at the note again. And then it happened. Maybe it was like a spasm, a reflex I couldn't control or didn't realize I was doing. More likely it was conscious, a taking born somewhere in memory.

It's mine, I heard some distant part of myself say. *It belongs to me too.*

When she turned around, I saw my one chance. I leaned down to pick up the note, shoved it back into the file, grabbed the file, and walked out the door.

"Bye."

"Call me when you get to court?" my mother called out after me.

"Sure, sure," I called back to her, walking quickly on the footpath from the house toward my car.

Even before I got to the sidewalk, I was already feeling bad about snatching it and running out the door with it like a delinquent child. I was an adult. What was I doing? "*He* won't throw anything away," I heard my mother repeat to herself. And then I imagined what he would probably say back to her, as he'd done, so many times before.

Es ken zein tzu nitz.

It could be of use some day, he'd say. It's a sin to throw away, to waste, something that could be of use one day. You never know. You never know what scarcity lies ahead.

But by the time I got to my car, I didn't feel so bad. I tossed the file onto the passenger seat and stared at it. He could have thrown it away, that file and whatever was inside. Why would he keep something like that? Why was there even a file with her name on it? He could have shredded it or burned it. Why wouldn't he get rid of the evidence? I drove for a bit, then parked on a side street, and in the car, I opened it. I could see there were some more notes, a postcard, and a few letters and photocopies.

I could only get myself to read that one note.

Do not share this with no one.
Keep this hidden.
Do you like my little hands? Don't they look like yours?

And like a bad déjà vu, that night, ten years ago, the sound of water, its echo in my head, the phone, heavy in my hand, was replayed, but now also underlined forever in that damn note.

Two

Later that afternoon, after work and at home in my bedroom, I reached into my bag and took out the file again, but thin, it slid out of my hands and landed with a kind of a weird smack onto the wood floor. I thought it would have spilled its contents on the floor, but it remained intact, as if it knew I wasn't sure I wanted to see whatever else was in it. It was just one of those standard manila folders you find in every Office Depot or Staples, cream-colored, with a wide tab. Old and yellowing now, the tab too was worn. I almost reached out to pick it up, but I didn't. And there it stayed, unopened on my floor, entreating and repelling me, and for a minute it almost looked like a secret trapdoor hidden under the rug of a creaky old house, like the kind I'd read about in those teen detective novels when I was twelve.

"Hi, Mama."

Talia appeared at my bedroom door, her iPod's paper-white wires drizzling down from her ears, and she sat down cross-legged on the rug. She was about to turn sixteen in a couple of short months. Even while sitting on the floor, her body arched upward into a dancer's carriage. I thought she looked more like David than me, but on the phone we sounded exactly alike, and I loved that callers very often couldn't tell us apart.

It was the end of a hot afternoon, June 2003. I'd come home from work more than an hour ago, and should have started dinner. But the courthouse, where I'd been a Juvenile Court judge for fifteen years, had stayed with me in the car on the way home. Even now in my bedroom, I could feel the weight of its windowless stretch of paneled rooms and the buzz-drone of attorneys, defendants, and jury pools in its long and speckled terrazzo hallways. And then there was that file. Dinner could wait.

"Talia, why didn't you tell me you were coming home late today?" I asked. Outside the window, twilight was creeping in slowly.

"But I did, Mom, this morning. I told you. Don't you remember? I called you when you were at work, and told you." Talia pulled out her earbuds and stood up. "And Dad said he would be late too, and Oren called to say he wouldn't be coming for dinner. And he also told me to tell you that he wasn't going to move back home until after graduation."

"You told me you were coming home late?"

"We had an extra two hours of practice."

"That's right." I remembered now.

"What's with you today?" She laughed. "Do you need a hearing test?"

"Nothing is with me." But she was right, even though it had nothing to do with hearing. Most of the time, I could even hear the soft whir of the generators underneath the courthouse and the tiny hum of the overhead fluorescent lights. But, like a bad cell phone connection, I'd only grasped parts of what she'd told me midmorning. It was that file, acting like a radio jammer in my head.

"What's that?" Talia asked, as though she'd read my mind, and pointed to the folder, still on the floor.

I pushed it away with my bare foot. "Nothing important," I said, but she looked at me unconvinced. "Just some old insurance papers," I added.

"Oh. Okay." Talia turned on the television in my bedroom.

An entertainment reporter was talking, but her words seemed swallowed up. Talia must have left a TV on in the den, and I could hear both sets in a strange time delay. The den was on the other side of the house, but the TV there somehow seemed to sound louder. "Can you turn off the TV in the den?" I asked her. She got up and was back in a minute. "That's better," I sighed.

"Next Sunday we have a competition in Long Beach. At two o'clock," Talia reminded me.

"Right, and what time—" I stopped. I suddenly saw the slim crack in the wall over my bed, a parting gift of the last minor earthquake, or was it a warning of some other earthquake to come? It needed fixing, along with a dozen other things in the house.

A couple of years back, we'd moved to this house in Encino, named for *los encinos,* the hundred-year-old California oak trees that dotted the hills. It was a so-called bedroom community in the center of the San Fernando Valley of Los Angeles and mostly in the foothills of the Santa Monica mountain range. The house was perched on a small knoll, sitting above the street that gushed with rivers of water when the winter rains came. It was what I liked best about the neighborhood—the uphills and downhills melting into one another.

Inside, everything was neat, too neat for some. Friends loved to give me a hard time, rib me about where I stashed the piles of mail, bills, and paperwork. But that's the way I liked it, almost needed it to be—a tamed interior horizon, no clutter, no china cabinets full of knickknacks like my parents.

I got up to turn on the AC. The entire week had been hot. Even the apricot tree outside my bedroom seemed to feel the lethargy of the summer solstice, the longest day of the year, only days away. Heavy with fruit, one of its branches had collapsed from the heat, and all over the yard, the apricots were soft and yielding into the color of ripe orange.

"Two o'clock, Mom," she repeated.

"Yes, yes. Got it."

Later, I drove Talia to her friend's house. Stopped at a red light, I looked at my daughter. Her long, brown hair ran down her back like dark syrup. She fidgeted in the car, pressing each one of the radio buttons in quick succession.

"I might be a little late," she said. "I have a lot to cover for my American history test tomorrow. "

I turned to look at her. She was already talking about applying to colleges out of state, and I could almost hear it already—the sound of a boarding announcement, and a jet taking off from LAX, taking her away.

"When do you want me to pick you up?"

"That's all right, I'm getting a ride back with Sammie's dad," she said, flipping through the American history textbook on her lap.

"Are you sure? I don't mind." More and more now, she wanted to sleep over at friends' houses, coming home wearing clothes I didn't recognize, T-shirts and jeans I hadn't bought for her.

"It's really okay," she said, smiling.

"What about dinner? I can make something for you when you get home," I offered.

"Sammie's mom is making dinner." Talia smiled.

"Okay, I get it."

Talia smiled again. "I'm bad with dates, Mom, not like you. You're good at remembering stuff, Mom, aren't you?"

"Good at remembering? I guess, maybe." Some things I remembered in perfect detail. But then others came to me in little fragments, spurts of memories triggered by a word or a sound, and they floated around in my head like motes, and then, just as quickly, disappeared.

"What date are you talking about?"

"November 22, 1963. You know, the date, in Dallas, when Kennedy was shot," she said.

"November 1963," I repeated. That was barely four months after my brother, Ron, was born, I remembered. I paused. "And she. She was so upset."

"Who? Who was upset?"

"Aunt Ree. It was like she'd lost another love of her life."

"Another love? Aunt Ree?" Talia looked up from her history book. "Didn't you used to say Aunt Ree was your favorite aunt, right?"

"She was, and that's what I used to call her when I was a little girl, Ree, short for Rhea. I'm not even sure where it came from or who told me to call her that. But that's what I called her.

"Mom?"

"But I don't call her Aunt Ree anymore, just Rhea."

"Mom?"

I thought about the file still sitting on my bedroom floor, and I made a quick mental note to put it away somewhere. Somewhere where I wouldn't have to see it.

"Mom? Mom, stop the car. We're here," Talia yelled out.

I was eleven. They'd dismissed school early on that Friday, but I didn't know why. I saw our Impala parked on the street, and I was surprised that it was my mother and not Aunt Ree who'd come to pick me up. The car was sky blue, but it looked pale and gray in the early afternoon light. When I climbed into the back seat, I heard the radio, loud, but there was another sound. My mother was crying. I looked out the window. It wasn't that cold for Philadelphia in November, but the street too looked wintry, the trees bare, and people seemed to be walking in slow motion past our car.

My mother drove me home. Aunt Ree came over later. And even though it was a Friday night, and we never watched TV on Shabbat, someone turned on the TV, and we all sat and watched the news. I'd never seen Aunt Ree cry before, and I watched her. Her tight bun was loose around the edges of her face, and her blue eyes red as she pulled out a handkerchief from under her wristwatch. But why did her eyes go back and forth from the screen to my father?

For hours that night, it was a blur of black and white, and again, the next day. And then the day after that too, the open car, the echo of shots, a woman's black veil, then horses pulling the caisson, and the coffin draped in an American flag. And as the caisson stopped on the street, Aunt Ree slipped out of the room.

Three

The next morning, I didn't sleep well and was up at dawn as the summer morning unwrapped slowly, shedding like thin layers of filmy gauze. I opened all the shutters to let in the light and turned off the entry light. When I opened the front door, I could already hear the sounds of a lawn mower, then a gardener's leaf blower, and hammers nailing shingles onto the roof of a house down the street. I closed the door. David was already dressed and making coffee in the kitchen, and he offered me a cup.

"Remember we're meeting the Freemans for dinner Saturday night," he reminded me.

I took the coffee and walked toward the back of the house to open the sliding doors. "Yes, yes, sure. I remember. But . . ." I paused. "Do we really have to go? Oren's graduation is coming up, our anniversary too. And I've got so many edits to do on the novel, and I've been so busy at work, and . . ." I stopped. "Can we just say no?"

I slid open the door. Even though there were no pine trees in our backyard, our neighbors' pines sat above us, and soft blankets of dry needles had fallen all over the patio. I took in the faint, waterless smell.

"Just say no? *No* falls right out of your mouth way too easily," David called out, and gave me a familiar, mostly annoyed, but partly amused look. He was so much better at social stuff than I. He had an easy way with people, an ability to make conversation and instant friendships wherever he went, even in short taxi and elevator rides. It took me longer to connect. But saying *no* wasn't just about connections with other people. It was a new skill I was trying to learn after years of thinking of myself as the accepting and overly compliant daughter. *No* had started to give me the power to decide what I wanted rather than what people wanted for and from me.

I came back to the kitchen. Today, David wore a freshly pressed shirt and an Italian tie that had belonged to his dad, Ben. Like Ben, who'd passed away only three years before, David wore his clothes well. But taller than his father, he'd only been able to inherit his dad's ties and silk pocket handkerchiefs, not the handmade shirts Ben had ordered for himself on his frequent trips to Milan or Ben's hand-tailored suits.

"And you? Maybe you say the word *yes* too often?"

He drank up the last bits of coffee in his cup and put the cup in the sink.

"Didn't we talk about this already? You said you would go. Let's leave it at that," he said, planting a kiss on my forehead and grabbing his wallet and keys. "I'm late. See you tonight."

"Well, okay. See you later," I said, but he was already out the door to the garage.

Later, I got into the car and turned on the engine. The radio came on loud. Last night Talia had reset my radio station to KIIS, but I didn't want to turn it back to my classical music station. Today, Talia's pop music station would keep me company on the way to work. It was already hot and I had to turn on the AC and roll up the windows while the car thumped with rap beats.

I was on my usual route to work, passing a power station where half a dozen homeless women navigated their shopping carts toward the entrance of a recycling plant, waiting for the chain-link gates to open. One blew me a kiss as I drove by, and I looked back at her. Rhea used to do that—blow a kiss into the air and fling her hand out. And although I hadn't seen her in years, I could still hear her voice, that tiny nasal inflection.

How's ma little girl doin' today? she'd say with a kind of sugary, Southern accent, even though she wasn't from anywhere near the South. But Rhea had a knack for being anyone from anywhere, a chameleon who sometimes appeared in elegant furs and jewels, and other times in drab cotton housecoats.

Two courthouses sat side by side within the confines of the Erwin Street Mall, a civic square containing a jumble of architectural styles, each building representing its own decade, and also housing the Van Nuys City Hall. The newer courthouse was a tall rectangle with a glassy face, its curvy half-circle rotunda jutting out of the entrance, almost as an afterthought, or an apology for its starkness. Behind the courthouse, silver-and-black Sheriffs' Department buses began to unload their cargo of defendants, and the rolling metal shutters clanged shut.

The east courthouse was the older of the two, a curvy, 1970s monolith, with a black lava rock facade that matched the parking structure nearby. Inside were pebbly terrazzo floors and old, sunburst clocks, and space age circles of fluorescent light beamed down from the hallway ceilings.

My courtroom was in the older building where every wood-paneled courtroom looked the same—long tables in the well, and the two rows of chairs in the jury box, along with the gunmetal filing cabinets and gray-and-white County of Los Angeles calendars tacked up on the walls. And in each, the California state seal floated above the judge like an exclamation mark.

I walked past the messy jumble of metal detectors and the clutter of makeshift security signs taped to the walls at the first-floor entryway and headed for the judges' elevator to take me to the third floor. Waiting for the elevator, I was feeling grateful. I loved my job, and getting the Van Nuys Juvenile Court assignment had been the culmination of my unusual and sometimes circuitous legal career, having graduated from law school in Israel, taken the California bar exam years later, written for a legal newspaper, worked at a couple of law firms, and then become a research attorney for a presiding Superior Court judge.

I opened the door to my courtroom from the back hallway. Magda and Beatrice, the two Spanish-speaking interpreters who were assigned to my court today, were already there, talking to each other. The court had interpreters for dozens of languages, interpreters for Arabic, Mandarin, Tagalog, Punjabi, and Korean, but the majority of full-time interpreters in Van Nuys interpreted for Spanish speakers. I loved listening in on their lively conversations and often joined them for lunch, feeling more at home with them than my mostly male judicial colleagues.

"In Mexico, they use *mirar*, to look, for everything. They rarely use *ver*, to see," Magda said to Beatrice. "It's very different in Spain," she continued, in Spanish tinged with Catalan. "There's definitely a difference, between to look and to see."

"For some reason, they use the word that shows intention, rather than the physical act of seeing," Beatrice weighed in.

"Yesterday, I had a witness respond to a question relating to seeing a child—*lo voy a buscar*," Magda continued. "I thought he meant, 'I am going to pick him up,' but it turned out the man wanted to say, 'I'm going to search for him.'"

"I don't know. I think growing up with two languages has always made me feel like I'm missing something, as though I don't quite fit into either one," Beatrice said, and Magda nodded her head in agreement.

I found myself nodding too. At home my parents and grandparents had spoken in a mix of English and Hebrew with a sprinkling of Yiddish and Romanian, and all through my childhood, I was also never sure which language or which world I quite fit into.

Just then, the bailiff entered the courtroom and seated the crowd. I zipped up the last inch of my black robe, took a deep breath, and put on my "judge face," the face that made me look confident and unflappable, even when I wasn't, the face that was supposed to be able to peel away layers of facts, truths, half-truths, and lies, along with a posture that kept argumentative lawyers probing for weakness at bay.

Magda explained the rights statement in Spanish and my morning session of thirty arraignments began.

~

Back in the car after work, I took another deep breath. My workday was over, but I didn't want to go straight home, not just yet. Anyway, David was working late, and Talia was at another dance rehearsal. As I drove, the late afternoon shadows seemed to slow everything down on the street, and I eased up on the accelerator. A large, dark sign stuck out from the sky on one of Ventura Boulevard's dull corners like a weird, dark stop sign: ANTIQUE MALL.

I made a quick left turn, parked the car on a side street, and walked in. Inside, the building looked like a co-op of antique shops, subdivided into numbered stalls, each crammed with armoires and display shelves uneven with memorabilia and kitsch.

At the entrance was a man with long, ice-white hair and a fancy cowboy shirt.

"Hi there, I'm Rick. Anything I can help you with today?" he asked, the pearl of his snap buttons exuding a strange opalescence in the dim light.

"I'm looking for . . . well, actually . . . just browsing."

I suddenly thought about the postcards David's mother had recently found and given to him a month ago. They'd been in a small stack, written by David's father years before. Ben had been away a lot on business, and the cards had been postmarked from all over the world—Venice and Alaska, Hong Kong and Caracas, Florida. Some of the photographs bled over the edges, others were framed with a white border.

"Maybe postcards. I'm looking for postcards," I finally sputtered out, almost a question.

"Are you a postcard collector?" he asked, then ushered me to the back of the shop to space number 144.

"No, not really."

My dearest David, each of the postcards began. In one from Washington State, his dad had promised to take him fishing one day in the Wenatchee River, but his father wasn't really a fisherman, and they never went on that trip.

Rick left me at the stall to sift through three plastic shoeboxes filled with cards. There were hundreds, glossy and colorful, mostly from vacation spots, postcards from motels and national parks, island paradises and European cities, monuments and churches. Each postcard was marked in pencil with a value based on the photograph and the age of the card.

Having a wonderful time, the phrase repeated itself on many of the cards. *Wish you were here.* After about forty minutes, I'd gone through most of the three shoeboxes, but I couldn't find any one I wanted.

I was still sifting through the last shoebox when Rick returned to the stall. "Found anything?" he asked, glancing at his watch. "Sorry, but I'm closing early today."

"Oh sorry. I'm almost done."

Rick was standing over me when I came across it. It was the postmark I saw first—April 21, 1942. April 21 was my father's birthday, and 1942 would have been the year he'd turned twenty-one. The postcard was smaller than the others in the shoebox, and very different from the rest, not a glossy souvenir from a trip. It was addressed in type to the donor of some sort of package, someone named W.H. Caldwell who lived in Brooklyn. Two pale red postage stamps of King

George VI, each valued at "1d," sat one alongside the other, a neat part dividing the king's perfect profile. Four kinds of flowers graced each corner of the stamps, all beneath the waves of a cancellation mark. I turned the postcard over. The paper was yellowing, but intact, the writing intriguing, almost musical.

Dear Sir,
Many thanks. I'll soon
be out of here now, then I shall
be lit up!
Yours Sincerely
Pte Maynard A.T.

And toward the bottom was something that had been preprinted, but strangely, part of the sentence had been underlined by hand in ink:

<u>Do not</u> <u>disclose</u> *any particulars of your unit.*

Rick said something to me, but I could barely hear him. I thought it was because of the rush of traffic on the street outside.

The handwriting was looping and deliberate, the ink welling up in certain letters, fading in others. On the left, a black-and-white sketch "by Grimes" depicted a soldier, a rifle strapped over his shoulder, wearing a long, cape-like coat as if on guard duty. He appeared to be standing in a puddle of water, smoking a cigarette, and a puff of smoke hovered above his head. Underneath the sketch was the caption *We're All Lit Up—Let Battle Commence*. I read the card over again. I liked the soldier's stab at humor, the exuberance of his exclamation point, the way he'd carved out seven lines from the smallest of spaces. His one comma was careful, unhurried, his capital "I" curling like a musical clef, his numbers crisp and precise, but it was something else that stood out—those three words that were underlined: *<u>Do not disclose</u>*.

"Hey, looks like that one there is the one you want," Rick said, checking his watch again. "Look, I really do have to close up."

"I wonder why he did that, underlined those words?" I turned to show Rick, but he was already walking toward the front of the store. Why the emphasis? Was it for humor's sake? Or was he speaking in code? Maybe it meant nothing.

I followed Rick to a vintage cash register where he rang up my purchase. "That'll be a whopping dollar and a half, miss," Rick said. "Come again when I don't have to close up early," he said and hurried me out the door.

A minute later, I was outside on the street with the postcard in my hand. I expected the noise of traffic, but there was none. There was only the sound of the deadbolt snapping into place as Rick locked the front door.

My father didn't talk about the war, and he didn't have numbers tattooed on his arm. He didn't tell me any stories about a ghetto or partisans hiding in forests. He'd only say that he'd been "there." But at night, "there" came into my pink room like the black-and-white trains of boxcars I'd seen on the news, and I was on that train, rushing across a dark landscape. But the train didn't get to its destination, falling off a cliff, exploding open just as it reached bottom, and I started to run into the woods, dogs barking behind me. If I could just get to where they were, it would be okay and I could help them too, I thought. I could help them, Sgt. Chip and 2nd Lt. Gil, the GIs from Combat. *I knew a little Yiddish, and I could be their German translator. I could help them kill the Nazis, and they would give me one of their helmets and keep me safe.*

I woke up, breathless and reached out to my doll. She was hung up on a nail, within my reach just above the headboard of my bed. She had a red, wide felt skirt with a zipper that opened, which was where I hid the silver dollars my grandfather had given me. There was also candy, for the road, and my little pearl ring, something I could sell. I didn't tell anyone I named her "Escape." She was there for me, only me, just in case. Just in case I needed to run away if I found myself "there," in the middle of the night.

Four

I came home and turned on the computer in my office.

April 21, 1942.

Enter.

That was Day 964 of World War II, a little less than three years into the war. The Battle of Britain had been raging since August of 1940, but the US had declared war on Germany and Japan barely five months before. Jews were already being systematically slaughtered all over Europe. But it would be three more years till Germany surrendered in May of 1945.

All this I knew, or thought I knew, generally. Still, the timeline, the length of the war and the Holocaust, 1933–1945, seemed staggering—twelve years from the time Adolf Hitler became chancellor of Germany until the Third Reich was crushed. It had been more than a decade of war, evil, and suffering.

I typed in "A.T. Maynard." Google ignored my periods and brought up links to "at Maynard," as if I was looking for a place, and not a person. But I soon discovered that the acronym RASC after the private's name, meant he'd been attached to the Royal Army Service Corps, and that he was British.

I tried MapQuest next, easily finding the Brooklyn return address, then zooming in and out on the street map, learning the address did still exist, then clicking several times on the aerial view.

Surfing the web, I found hundreds of queries for lost comrades and friends, searches for people lost. They seemed like tiny distress signals, other people also chasing ghosts.

An hour later and I hadn't logged off. I looked at the postcard on my desk again. It had absolutely nothing to do with me. Maynard was a complete stranger. Except for the postmark, the date of my father's twenty-first birthday, there were no obvious connections to me, no Caldwells or Maynards in my Eastern European Jewish gene pool, no close associations with Brooklyn or London, not even any smokers in my family. There were really no good reasons to spend my time trying to search for him. But why had the soldier underlined those three words? Was he poking fun at the authorities, or did he have something to hide? Could it be an odd cry for help, or recognition? What else besides the "particulars of your unit" did he need not to disclose?

I sat back in my office chair. One of the leather armrests was torn, the stuffing beneath poking through, and I tried to nudge it back in, but it popped right out again. One more thing that needed to be fixed, that I needed to fix. Waiting for me was the broken sprinkler, which had to be replaced, and the pull on the sliding screen door, which had lost a screw and was barely attached.

The telephone rang, and it was Oren. His friend had invited him to go on a trip to South Africa in December, he told me. "And I'll have to have a layover in London," he explained.

"Sounds great," I said, waiting for more details, but Oren didn't say much more.

"When exactly?"

"Not sure."

"When do I see you?"

"Not sure. Soon. We can talk all about it later," he said, and hung up.

"Mom, what are you doing?" Talia called out from her bedroom.

I hadn't realized Talia had come home.

"Just messing around on the computer," I said, and walked over to her bedroom to show her the postcard. I looked at the bright blue IKEA clock in her room, motionless at 8:50 because Talia had long ago insisted I not change the dead battery. "I like the clock but hate that ticking sound," she'd said, and I'd let it go. There was something comforting about a clock frozen in time.

I showed her the postcard. "What if I could find the man who wrote this?" I asked.

She glanced at the postcard. "But why would you do that?" she asked.

"I don't know. I thought it might be—"

"Watch this," she said. "We learned this great move today." She started to do a short segment of a jazz routine her coach had recently choreographed. I watched her arms fly forward, then swivel into a fall, collapsing on the floor.

"That's great," I said, but it was the thought of finding Private Maynard that flew around in my head.

"You're not watching."

"Sorry. Do it again. Maybe I could give it back to him, or his family." I'd been thinking about it all afternoon, but saying it out loud seemed to transform the weird thought into a promise, but to whom? It didn't seem right for me to keep it. Somehow, it had migrated from London to Brooklyn, then found its way to some thrift store in the San Fernando Valley, but it belonged somewhere else, with someone else. "Maybe I could fix this."

"Fix what?"

"I mean, maybe I could return it."

I walked back to my office and Talia followed me.

"That's nice, Mom," she said, turning on the TV in my office surfing the channels. Talia could easily watch three different programs at one time, flipping back and forth between channels during the commercials. She finally settled on MTV, a rerun of a *Real World* all-day marathon, and watched for a bit, then went back to her room.

When she left, I muted the TV and went back to my computer screen.

Back on the web, I found the War Graves Commission, a database listing almost two million men and women of the Commonwealth forces who died during the two world wars, and over twenty thousand cemeteries, memorials, and other locations worldwide where they were commemorated. I typed in Maynard's name on the search engine.

Here are the results of your enquiry.

There were dozens of Maynards who had the rank of private, but none matched the serial number on the postcard or the regiment. I typed in his name and serial number again, just to be sure.

From what I could see, it looked like he hadn't been killed during World War II.

There was still a chance he was alive.

Scrolling through the other names, though, I saw hundreds who hadn't survived. There were pages of them, listed by rank, service, date of death, age, regiment, nationality—graves in Dunkirk, Egypt, Italy, Malaysia, and Palestine.

"Actually, I do think you could do it." Talia suddenly reappeared and made a Martha Graham–like stance, elongated and motionless in the air. "Find that British private," she continued, arms outstretched in the air. "I think you could do it. If anyone could, it would be you, Mom."

There was a music video now on my TV. The still-muted video flashed in seconds from scene to scene, like snippets of metallic fabric cut and stitched together. The camera zoomed in and out, a close-up followed by a panoramic view. The dancers dipped in a V-formation, storming the camera, and Talia strutted and slinked with them, her shoulders shimmying up, then pressing down in syncopation.

"I mean it. I really think you can do it."

Talia peered at me then suddenly rose on one leg, switching seamlessly from hip-hop to ballet, completing a perfect arabesque, her other leg extending in a straight line, motionless.

I didn't know a house could have a name till Aunt Ree drove us to Ivy Hall, the name of Madame Florence Cowanova's Philadelphia mansion where she taught ballet. I looked for the ivy, but there wasn't any, only a big house with red bricks and lots of chimneys.

Inside, there was a ballroom with shiny wooden floors lined with ballet barres, a painted ceiling, and a big chandelier in the middle. But my tutu was too tight around my waist, and my arabesques were bad. And Madame walked around with a stick that she tapped first on the floor, then to the back of our necks when Dena and I didn't stand up straight, I complained to Aunt Ree.

"Now, girls, don't cha want to grow up and be like Grace Kelly and marry a prince?" Aunt Ree asked us as she pointed to one of the framed photographs of Madame's past pupils on the walls of the stairs that led to the ballroom.

"I do, but—" It seemed impossible to be like the beautiful lady in the photo.

"Aw, c'mon. You can do anything you want to do, girls," she said. And Dena and I just looked at each other.

Dena was Aunt Ree's little girl. Blonde, her skin was as white as Aunt Ree's pearl necklace. Although four years younger than me, she was my playmate and best friend. "Let's pretend," we whispered to each other when we made tents out of furniture and sheets on quiet Shabbat afternoons, when we couldn't drive anywhere, and my parents

23

took their usual afternoon nap. Outside, we made a makeshift kitchen around a large oak tree in my front yard. Later we tried to catch fireflies on hot summer nights, just before we looked for and counted three stars.

"It's over, it's over," we shouted in unison. But my grandfather came out to make sure we really saw them, those shterin, *he called them, those three perfect stars that meant the Shabbat was over and we could finally turn on the TV.*

Five

The next day, the valley was overcast, a pressure of low clouds, and the clouds seemed to creep into the house, muting everything. I was about to leave for the courthouse when I called out to David, but he didn't hear me. I called out again; then I found him in the den and showed him the postcard. He held it up to the light.

"What do you think?" I asked.

"Interesting for sure."

"But what do you think about his writing?"

"His writing looks a little shaky, maybe a little labored?"

"Are you sure?" His analysis surprised me.

"I don't know. I feel a little sad for him."

"Sad? Hmmm. What about his sense of humor, right here?" I pointed to the second line of the postcard. "He wrote, *I'll soon be out of here now, then I shall be lit up*, referring to the caption, *We're all lit up*, underneath the sketch of a soldier. Sad, really?" But the word *sad* crept over me.

"People show pain in different ways," he said, handing the post-card back to me.

"Guess that's true."

"Do you think I'm completely crazy to do this, to try to find him?" I asked.

He shook his head and laughed. "Not at all. I love the way your brain is always working on overtime."

"I'm not sure that's actually a compliment," I said, but I laughed too.

"Well, most of the time. But stop second-guessing yourself," he said. "And you remember about Saturday?"

"Saturday?"

"The Freemans. Dinner. Seven thirty."

"It's for sure?" I hadn't forgotten. But a few hours on Saturday night would have been great to get some extra research on the post-card, I quickly calculated.

"For sure."

I looked at him. He was waiting for me to confirm, and I knew I was just being a pain in the ass now.

"Right. Okay, okay, seven thirty Saturday."

~

At work, the courthouse was abuzz with rumors about a new presiding judge and possible changes in assignments. Everyone was talking about how he was a stickler about certain things, and he wasn't a fan of judges doing "outside" activities, even though there weren't any specific ethical prohibitions. The rumors left me wondering if I should start worrying about losing my assignment in Van Nuys. For years before, I'd slogged downtown via the always-congested 101, and the assignment to the Van Nuys courthouse, the courthouse closest to my home, had been a game changer for me. It had allowed me to be more present for my children, and it was a posting I couldn't jeopardize.

But I put my worries aside for the time being.

A vandalism case was last on the morning docket. A fourteen-year-old defendant pled guilty to defacing a storefront, and it seemed like it would be a simple clear-cut case until his mother asked to speak. Just a few months earlier, the boy had been the one who had found his father lying in a pool of blood, dead from a gunshot on the street, his mother explained, and since then he'd been on a tear of party-going, then tagging.

"To hide his grief he pretends that he is happy. He goes to parties and covers up his feelings," the mother continued, and her words struck a chord with me. Later, back in my chambers, I thought about the fourteen-year-old and then Private Maynard. If David was right, had the soldier also hidden his grief behind his cheerful words? Was he hiding his true self somehow? There was so much more to know, to piece together from the tiny fragment I'd found, and I took the postcard with me and walked over to the Van Nuys branch library across the street from the courthouse at lunchtime.

This parcel is presented through the Over-Seas League Tobacco Fund was printed on the left-hand side of the card. It took only a bit of digging online to discover that the postcard was a "response" card, included with requests to collect cigarettes for British and Free French soldiers, and organized by the Over-Seas League Tobacco Fund. A fragment of a British war relief solicitation letter appeared on a military memorabilia website. *I am sure your sympathies will be with the fighting men of Britain . . . we are doing all we can to send good cheer to the splendid lads who are fighting. . . .*

There were dozens of sites with references to Maynard's regiment, the RASC, some maintained by former veterans. One explained that "the RASC delivered all the food and ammunition to the front lines, also looking after all the transport, delivering gasoline. In other words, they were the mother regiment supplying all the other regiments with what they needed. We weren't based anywhere. When the infantry went . . . we went up behind with all the supplies."

I read on, learning that the British Ministry of Defense was strict on releasing any details, and although WWI army service records were now public, WWII records were still confidential.

I then emailed someone I found on a WWII memories project on the internet. Surprisingly, I got a response back from him almost immediately. His name was Bert, short for Albert, he'd emailed me from Melbourne, Australia, and we chatted back and forth.

I'm seventeen hours ahead of you in Los Angeles. You could say I'm writing to you from the future, he quipped. Nineteen forty-two was the year Bert enlisted at seventeen, he wrote. He'd just turned seventy-eight, he added, and he'd also tried but had trouble tracking down people who had served in the RASC.

He might be one of the many thousands who emigrated and started families after the war in Canada, South Africa, New Zealand, or Oz. We all came home from the war with itchy feet. Even if the private is still alive, he could be anywhere.

The piano recital was in a big house in Main Line Merion, owned by a woman composer who knew my father and had helped him write his master's in music thesis. As we walked up to the entrance of the mansion, my father told me that this house too had a name. It's called Dragon Hill, he said, and I stopped short at the gate. Dragon? But there are no real dragons here, he said, and took my hand and led me down the long, gravel driveway and around a fountain.

Inside, the recital room seemed enormous with a giant wall hanging of unicorns and beasts. Two pianos faced each other. I was barely seven, my hair slicked back in a ponytail and barrette. I was second to play on the long program, my sweaty hands pounding out two beginner pieces, the first, the tom-tom-like sounds of "From a Wigwam." At the end, there was a polite hum of applause, and my father said I had to go back to sit in the audience and listen to all the other pupils play. But I was sure I spotted him, the dragon, peeking out from up in the balcony, and I wanted to be anywhere, anywhere but there.

Six

After my last case of the day, I thought I'd surprise my parents with a visit and drove to the city. I wasn't sure whether I was still feeling a little guilty about absconding with the file the other day or just wanted to feel out whether my mother had noticed it was missing. Maybe both. I made a turn off Olympic Boulevard onto their street in the South Carthay section of Los Angeles, the street lined with Spanish-style houses built in the late 1920s and '30s and now designated a historic preservation overlay zone. Just as I turned, I spotted my mother. She seemed to be singing to herself as she rolled a black bin filled with trash out to the alley.

"Leora? This is a nice surprise. But didn't you tell me you had an appointment after work?"

I thought for a moment. "Appointment? Oh yes, it was canceled."

I'd forgotten I'd talked to her in the morning when she'd called, as she usually did, promptly at eleven, to check up on my plans for the day. We were the smallest of families, my father, an only child, my mother, who had one sister, my brother, and I. Protective of her tiny brood, my mother always needed to know our exact whereabouts, our comings and goings, and over the years, she'd become our traffic controller, alert to the location blips of her son and daughter, granddaughter and grandson on her own internal radar screen. Partly annoying, often endearing, that need for knowing where everyone was at all times was already starting to bubble up in me with my own children.

It was six o'clock, but the sun was still bright, lighting up the terra cotta tiles of the roofs on Alvira Street, a world and lifetime away from Haifa, where my mother, Yael, had been born in 1927 to Meir Hornstein and Chinka Shalit during the British Mandate for Palestine. Meir, born in Tulchin, Ukraine, in August 1898, had been an engineer in the Russian army who'd emigrated to Palestine after the Russian pogroms of the early 1920s. Chinka was from Kishinev, part of a family with musical roots. My mother's great-uncle David Moshe Steinberg, also originally from Kishinev, was a well-known cantor. Another great-uncle was said to have sung at La Scala Milan on the same playbill as world-renowned Russian singer Feodor Chaliapin.

I looked at the five additional trash bags already piled near the bin. Retired now from her job as an assistant at the Jewish Federation, my mother was still working on her cleanup campaign.

"Come, come in. Have you eaten?" I followed her up the steps to the house and into the foyer.

Inside, the living room was still in an unusual uproar, a racket of papers and boxes, and even more files strewn everywhere. Normally, the house was quiet, with the acoustics of an insulated sound studio and the doors to the bedrooms hushed shut, but today all the doors were thrown wide open, even the closets, with buckets of water and bottles of cleaning materials scattered about. Next to the old, upright piano my mother used to play, sadly idle now for years, was the shredder she'd recently bought at Staples, and a two-foot hill of ragged paper nearby.

"I can't stand all this stuff anymore. We don't need it, and I don't want it," my mother said, impatient to finish off the day's purges. Despite the day's exertions, she still looked cool and unruffled, and she wore her delicate Wittnauer bracelet watch which she usually kept in a heart-shaped box on top of her dresser.

Except for the papers and boxes, the Spanish-style house was exactly the same as it had been for all the more than fifteen years they'd lived in California.

In the living room was a floor-to-ceiling breakfront with all the bric-a-brac and family heirlooms my parents had accumulated over the years. The prized possessions were the gilded cup and saucer we used as Elijah's cup every Passover. A family legend recounted that a Russian czar had given them to a paternal great-grandfather for donating money to a hospital. There were hostess plates with scenes from famous operas, various stones from all over the world, and family photos from schools, graduations, and weddings. To the right was the formerly Spanish-style fireplace that had been covered over with travertine by a previous owner in the '80s. Bamboo plants in Chinese pots sat atop the hearth of the unused fireplace.

My father's office was just past a hallway lined with his family photos, as well as photos of himself in concerts and shaking hands with famous people. The office, where he retreated for hours, was a catacomb of books on Judaica, multiple sets of the Talmud, and prayer books that lined the wall behind his massive wooden desk. Another wall was packed with plaques of recognition, his awards, certificates, and framed diplomas.

In the dining room was the same mahogany set we'd had in Philadelphia. The silver was kept in a matching glass cabinet with a collection of family Kiddush cups, Hanukah menorahs, candlesticks, a snuffbox, and Torah pointers, all polished and gleaming. Every piece had a story or a memory attached to it. Each was carefully placed and then replaced in its designated spot after its use on a holiday.

"So much more to do here," my mother said, dusting off a ceramic figurine. "But we shall overcome." She looked up at the beams on the ceiling of the living room. "It's a beautiful room, isn't it?" It had taken her three years and viewing hundreds of houses for sale before she'd settled on this house in Carthay, one of her main concerns being that there should be a window in every room, even the bathrooms. She was very proud of it. It was also the first time she'd finally been the mistress of her own house, as my grandparents, who had lived with us for many years in Philadelphia and Saint Louis, had both passed away.

"It *is* beautiful," I said.

"I like your hair up that way," my mother said, eyeing my ponytail. "Away from your face." Her hair was short and very straight, as it had been for years, and probably part of the reason I liked to keep my wavy and sometimes unruly hair shoulder-length.

"Yeah, something different today."

"You should always wear it up like that," she said and continued her shredding.

There were other furnishings my parents had brought with them from the East Coast, some hand-me-downs from what we all called the "Big House," Rhea's stately, stone colonial on Raynham Road in the posh Main Line section of Philadelphia, and I wondered whether my mother was getting rid of those things too.

"So, what's new, Leora?"

"Not much."

"But I see something is on your mind." It was more a statement than a question.

"Not much."

"I can tell. Something is wrong. Tell me," she said.

"Nothing's wrong, really."

"Is David's work okay?"

"Everything is fine."

She shrugged. "You'll tell me when you're ready. Did you arrange a new carpool for Talia?" she asked.

"Not yet."

"What are you waiting for?"

I leaned down to pick up a Chinese-style bowl off the floor. "Want some help?"

"No need. Just leave that there," my mother said, pointing.

Just then my father appeared. He wore a short sleeve shirt, a little frayed at the collar. He'd once been a fastidious dresser, but lately he'd seemed to double down on wearing his most worn-out clothes. Long gone were the studded tie clips and the monogrammed pocket squares peeking up from his suit jacket.

He greeted me with a bear hug.

"Ah . . . Leora . . . is here," he said, almost in a whisper, holding me in a quick tight embrace, but then letting go just as quickly and step-ping away. He'd always been a hard worker, never saying no to any extra job offered to him. But he'd had a stroke three years ago and, having nixed a recommendation for a speech therapist, was working and talking less and less. His bass baritone voice used to boom with perfect diction, and it saddened me to hear his voice now sounding like the soft hiss of a dying light bulb.

There was a long trail of legacies and history in his voice. He had been born Levi Isaac, the only child of David Halperin from Kishinev, now Chisinau, Russia, and Rachel Wahrman of Iasi, Romania, both from well-known rabbinic families. David's great-grandfather, Jacob Joseph Halperin, had been an important banker and head of the firm Halperin and Sons. He was so influential that when in 1843, the Tsarist Russian government sponsored a small conference of dis-tinguished Jews in St. Petersburg to resolve a bitter dispute among Jewish groups about modernizing Jewish education, Jacob Joseph was one of the five distinguished Jews present. But his anti-Hassidic opponents eventually discredited him in the eyes of the authorities, which led to his financial ruin and a debtors' prison.

David and Rachel were married in the small town of Pirlita, a vil-lage in Moldavia. The young couple lived in Kishinev for a time, but after the Russian Revolution, the Jews of Kishinev were in danger, and my grandmother Rachel dressed up as a man, sewed her small cache of diamonds into the man's overcoat she wore, and fled Russia, returning to her father's home in Iasi. My father was born there, in Iasi on April 21, 1921, and grew up like a prince, doted on, coddled, and dressed in velvet and lace. In Iasi, the extended maternal family lived together in a large compound, which included a synagogue, apartments for aunts, uncles, and cousins, a basement for food storage, and an outhouse. It was presided over by Rachel's father, Rabbi Meshulam Wahrman from Foltechen, and Leah Derbarimdicker, the great-granddaughter of the renowned Hasidic Rabbi Levi Isaac of Berdichev, of whom many stories and books had been written. Although deeply Orthodox, family photos showed the women dressed in the fashion of their times, beautiful 1920s and '30s satin ensembles with fashionable short hairstyles and big bows. At some point, Rachel, David, and my father moved to the capital, Bucharest, where there were a hundred thousand Jews, 10 percent of the city's population. There my father attended secular school as well as yeshiva and then later Bucharest University. Their life revolved around family, friends, the synagogue, and music, with trips back to Iasi and seaside holidays. Both my grandfather and father served as cantors. Then Hitler came to power in Nazi Germany.

"So," he said, "tell me something new."

There were flowery carpets at the Big House, heavy, silver cigarette lighters on the end tables, a foot buzzer under the dining room to summon the butler, and a maid dressed in a crisp white uniform and black apron. Aunt Ree was married to Sol. He was very rich, everyone said, and Aunt Ree hosted small parties and get-togethers there, some in the back garden where there was a fishpond and hammocks and lawn chairs for guests to lie on.

But Sol died when Dena was two. Why does she sit next to my father at the Seder table? I asked my grandmother. It's just a little kindness, my grandmother explained. She's so little and fatherless, my grandmother said. Zies a yosem. She's an orphan now.

Aunt Ree later moved back to a smaller house, but she managed to salvage some of the cut-glass brandy decanters and the cigarette lighters from the bigger house. This house had a sour cherry tree in the front yard and a ceramic burro on the front pathway. And even though there were no other pools in the neighborhood of simple, two-story houses, Aunt Ree decided she wanted a full-sized swimming pool. Like they have in California, she explained, and one day, the bulldozer came to dig out the earth, the pool reaching out to the ends of her back property.

We swam there, all of us, my mother too, in the blue-green pool, a tall hedge behind us. Dena and I sat on the edge of the pool in the matching bathing suits Aunt Ree had bought for us, arms around each other and grinning for the camera.

Seven

An hour later, I was still in my parents' living room. My mother was still working on the boxes. My father was sitting near the window.

"What's this thing? My mother asked, holding up a small, chipped teacup. "I have no idea where it came from," she continued. "This has to go," she said, putting it down on the floor.

"No, no," my father called out.

"But look at it. It's broken," she insisted.

He made a face. "I can fix it with glue."

"Glue won't help it. Where did you find it? On one of your walks in the neighborhood?"

"Do what you want." He surrendered and sat down on the sofa.

I wondered again whether my mother knew about the file I'd filched. I'd also started wondering whether I should share the file with my brother. Like me, my brother had also had a special relationship with Rhea. She'd doted on him, buying him gifts and bringing him along with her to the laundry she'd taken over from her ex-husband, Max, when my parents had declined to send Ron to summer camp.

I surveyed the living room floor. "Why don't you just have a big garage sale?" I asked. It was taking her weeks to sift through the junk in their house. A lawn sale would easily take care of all the knick-knacks, the mismatched china.

"But you see what he does. *He* won't throw anything away," she repeated, shooting my father a look.

In a vase in the living room were long-stemmed sunflowers. Wide and yellow, like bright faces, they reminded me of my favorite photo of my mother, tucked away in one of the photo albums. She was sixteen in the photo, wearing a peasant blouse embroidered with little Xs and posing in a field of giant sunflowers, but the photo didn't tell the entire story. My mother saw me looking at the flowers. "They're the color of corn. How I loved corn on the cob. But I couldn't even buy it then, when they used to sell it on the beach in Tel Aviv. You could smell it everywhere on the beach. It made me so hungry, but I couldn't afford even that, a small piece of corn, can you imagine that?"

"What was it like for you . . . in 1942?"

"Nineteen . . . forty . . . two?" She said the year slowly, emphasizing each digit. "That was just before my father died."

I knew the story. When my mother was fifteen, her father inexplicably died from a complication of a routine appendectomy, leaving behind my mother, her younger sister, Aliza, barely eight years old at the time, and a grieving and destitute thirty-nine-year-old widow, my grandmother Chinka. My mother was forced to leave high school and take up work at a salt factory and then a pharmaceutical company, and her younger sister was sent to a faraway boarding school. My mother did eventually finish high school, joining the Labor Youth Movement and later the Haganah, but she never got over her father's early and unexpected death.

"Just before he died," she repeated. "So young. Too young." She sighed.

"I know. That must have been so hard for you," I said.

"But what exactly did you want to know?"

"Did you know any British soldiers then, during that time, under the British Mandate?" I asked.

"British soldiers?" She thought a moment. "Not really. Some of the girls I knew went out with them, but not me. We called them 'poppies' because of their red berets. They liked to go to the bars near the beach. I was in a special underground unit that hid rifles from the British authorities in *slikim*, secret arms caches." She paused for a moment. "Those were the days," she said, and sighed again. "But why this question?"

"Oh just—" I said, and I told her about finding the postcard and about my idea of trying to find the British private.

"Find a British private?" my father suddenly piped in. "Why would you do that?"

Why? I couldn't think of an answer that would make any sense to him, but my mother seemed to somehow understand. "Oh, I see now," she said. She had a look I'd seen before, a flash of recognition, a fast-forward into the future that played in her head.

"What's going on with you?" she asked.

"I'm fine."

"Something else is going on? I can hear it in your voice."

"Everything's all right, really."

"Are you sure?"

"Yes," I pronounced with all the certainty I could rally.

"And Oren and Talia?"

"They're doing well. Stop worrying, Mom."

"Don't lose sight of things. Don't do what I did. Then suddenly it's too late. You can never make up the time. And David? He's good? Not coming back too late from the office, I hope, Lee-*ora*?"

I knew that when my mother emphasized the end of my name, it meant her antennae were up. I hated my mother's sixth sense, her ability to read between the lines. I always seemed to be in her perfect sights. She was always on the lookout for the signs of betrayal, from everyone, even from David, whom she adored, and from me, even when there were none. But I had betrayed her—that file that I had poached from their house. If she knew, she didn't let on.

"I'm going to the kitchen to get something to drink." My father stood up and stepped out of the room.

"You shouldn't spoil your children, you know." My mother turned to me. "They should know . . . they should know that nothing comes easy. I grew up without a father and with a mother who fell apart after he died. I had to learn to take care of myself."

"I don't spoil them."

I could hear the refrigerator open and close. She looked toward the kitchen. "You know I stayed with your father for your sake, and for your brother."

"But we didn't ask you to do that. We weren't children when we learned the truth. We were adults. You didn't have to stay with him."

My mother shook her head. "You can't understand me, Leora. Your father went back to Philadelphia, you know, for *her* funeral."

"I know. But that was two years ago, Mom."

"Yes, two years ago, ten years ago. Do you think it doesn't still hurt? I wish . . . I wish you could understand me."

"But I do understand you. Look, I just dropped by to say hello. I really have to go now."

"Sure. Come and go. Come and go. You can't stay for dinner?"

"I'm sorry, you know, the traffic is so bad going back to the valley."

"Yes, of course, the traffic," she mumbled to herself, and then went back to a box she'd been working on.

"I'll come out . . . with you . . . out to the car," my father said, returning from the kitchen.

I watched him carefully walk the two steps up from the sunken living room. There was much I didn't know about him, only parts of his story of survival that I'd pieced together over the years. Romania, an ally of Nazi Germany, was the first country in Europe to enact anti-Jewish statutes modeled after the Nuremberg Laws. Between 1938 and '39, citizenship was withdrawn from about 50 percent of the Jewish population of Romania, and between 1940 and '41, the Jews were expelled from all public and government sectors including the army. Observance of religion was restricted, Jews were prohibited from burying their dead in Jewish cemeteries, and marriages between Jews and Romanians were banned. On September 6, 1940, the Iron Guard, with the support of Germany and renegade military officers led by the Fascist premier, General Ion Antonescu, forced King Carol to abdicate. Antonescu imposed even stricter anti-Semitic laws and restrictions, deporting hundreds of thousands of Jews to concentration camps.

Bucharest was the scene of the Legionnaires' rebellion against Antonescu where leather-clad "Greenshirts" roamed the streets on motorcycles looking for Jewish victims, looting, killing, and burning homes in Bucharest's Jewish quarter, Vacaresti. Jews were plucked off the streets and beaten, tortured, and mutilated. Others were rounded up to sweep streets, clear snow, and remove the dead and wounded from the debris of bomb attacks. "Romanization" of assets continued, including expropriations of land, shops, goods, factories, and clothes, and the imposition of extra taxes.

But my father's family was lucky. Once he told me that he would never forget the day when the man who lived downstairs told his father not to go to the synagogue that morning. He was a restaurant owner and officially a Fascist, but my father's family were very well loved in the neighborhood. That day, the first twelve people who showed up at the synagogue were shipped to an abattoir and butchered.

The family escaped to the countryside and hid out with relatives for a while. When they returned to Bucharest, my father was rounded up and sent with three thousand others to the Cotroceni work camp in the suburbs of Bucharest where he became the unofficial Jewish chaplain of the camp. The conscripts built army training camps and rifle ranges, but had nothing to work with but their bare hands and some shovels. Some were allowed to live at home, reporting to work at five in the morning, and the camp commander, Colonel Agapiescu, displayed more humanity than other camp commanders, allowing sometimes for reduced work schedules. But although conditions were not as harsh as other labor camps, every week their hands were examined. Anybody without blisters was sent to the death camps of Transnistria.

He was also sent to other forced day labor camps in Poligon and Mogosoaia, where Jews would haul rocks and clear snow. Later, Jews in Bucharest continued to fare better than their counterparts in other regions of Romania, surviving in greater numbers. As an "ally" of the Nazis, the Romanians were given some official leeway to "deal with their Jews," and the Romanian government, known for corruption and graft, offered certain Jews living in Bucharest with specific professions or academic degrees a path to buy their way out of forced labor.

Teodore Stanescu, a professor my father knew at the Bucharest University, signed monthly documents called labor exemption certificates that allowed my father and other Jewish students to work in the Statistics Institute, where they were charged with compiling dictionaries, a blessing of sheer luck but one that left behind it the curse of survivor's shame.

On April 4, 1944, the Allies bombed Bucharest, and although their principal target was the train station, strong winds deflected bombs to other parts of the city, leaving over three thousand dead, including my grandmother's sister.

"I had to go to Rhea's funeral," my father said, when we got to my car, and in the outdoor light, I saw that his dark brown eyes were still flecked with saffron yellow. "Rhea was . . . she did so much for us . . . despite everything," he said, ticking his words off carefully, equally, like a metronome.

"I know. You did the right thing to go to her funeral, even Mom knows that."

"You think so?"

I looked at my father closely. He almost never phoned me, content with debriefing my mother after one of her calls to me, or sometimes even listening in on our conversations from an extension in another room. Rarer still was his asking my opinion.

"I think you did."

My father lingered at the door of my car. "I have to live with this now," he said, shaking his head. "That's the way it is. *Kacha ze*," he said in Hebrew. "It is what it is." He sighed and shut the car door for me.

My grandparents, David and Rachel, came to America to live with us when I was seven. My grandfather was a deeply religious man with a short, neatly trimmed white beard, who prayed every morning. But he also planted bulbs in the garden and made sweet grape and cherry wine in the basement and read the Yiddish Forward *newspaper. He also always made time to play with me. He taught me checkers first, then chess, and in between, the words of the morning and evening prayers, and he gave me silver dollars for birthdays and holidays. Best of all, every autumn, he put together the* sukkah, *the small hut that was topped with branches mixed with sky, and where shadows and light found their way to the walls made of sheets for the week of the Festival of Booths.*

My grandmother, short and wide, didn't like any kind of play, but my grandfather adored her, and called her koshkaleh, *his "little bird" in Yiddish. Once a month, he cut her hair and brought her slices of apples arranged like a flower on a plate.*

In the morning she pinned a tidy blue apron to her robe, and adjusted the matching blue kerchief on her head. Our kitchen was her domain once she came down the stairs to do the day's cooking. I stayed far away on the days she plucked and poured salt over the chickens to kosher them, or ground her own beef, only venturing in when she baked her chocolate babkas. When she was done, she'd close all the curtains in the living room.

"So the sun doesn't ruin the furniture," she insisted when I complained, and climbed back up the stairs to her bedroom to rest and read her Romanian romance novels.

One afternoon, I went upstairs and sat on the edge of her bed. Nearby was a chest of drawers with photos. There was one of me, one of Dena in softly hand-colored black-and-white. "He's my one and only son," my grandmother complained when I asked her why she'd left Israel to come to America. "My only child. When he was born, they had to use forceps. Forceps! Forceps!" she repeated.

"What are forceps?" I asked.

"You should never know. And when your father was little, he almost died of scarlet fever. But what could I do?" she whispered.

"What could you do about what?" I asked, a little loud, and she shushed me.

"Quiet, your father is taking a nap. He needs his sleep. Listen to me, we had to come. Es ez vus es iz." It is what it is, she said in Yiddish. "We had to come to America to save it—to save your parents' marriage."

Eight

*N*o one was home when I returned from the city, and I turned on all the lights. I sat down at my desk and dug out the Rhea file. I opened it up and glanced at the first note again, but then closed the file up, shoving it back into the bottom drawer of my file cabinet.

Instead, I took out a photocopy of the postcard I'd made from my desk drawer and tacked it up on the bulletin board I'd bought and hung up above the desk. My office was beginning to look like something out of an old TV cop show—stacks of papers on the floor, articles and photos thumbtacked to the cork. All that was missing was a link chart with string, connecting suspects and locations.

I looked at the photocopy again. This time I saw something I hadn't noticed before. On top, an octagonal censor's mark in pink, a crown, and the word "passed." In the middle, a round postmark was stamped South Tottenham, N.15, and postmarked April 21, 1942, 7:15 p.m. I wondered how long it took for the card to reach Caldwell in Brooklyn during wartime—a month, two?

I contacted a philatelist who explained that lighter stamp colors were used during World War II in order to economize on ink.

The card is correctly franked for surface mail to the USA from Great Britain. The red censor marking is a standard marking. Postcards were easy to censor because they did not require opening and resealing. The red mark merely says that a censor looked at the card and found nothing objectionable.

I then posted a query on the British Legion, an organization that provided financial, social, and emotional support to British veterans. Its website contained a "Lost Trails" link, where service friends could search for old colleagues and comrades.

Looking for Private A.T. Maynard (or next of kin) who served with RASC in World War II. Please contact.

I posted a similar message on genealogy.com, on the "Maynard Family Genealogy Forum," and sifted through some of the over three thousand messages already up on the site. I found websites that explained British Army military organization, and I tried to understand the relative sizes of corps, regiments, battalions, brigades, and divisions. I read up on military hierarchy, following the flowchart of ranks from private to brigadier.

On the internet, I found images of similar thank you postcards from other British soldiers, but most didn't include their army serial numbers. Some didn't even include their names. One postcard I found merely signed off "from a Lancashire lad." Most interesting was the fact that none of the others I'd found had any underlining below that same admonition—*Do Not Disclose.*

Why did Maynard include his serial number and the name of his unit? Did he hope Caldwell would write him back? Was he hoping for a correspondence with his donor, and if so, did Caldwell ever reply?

In the meantime, I got a reply from the Royal Logistics Corps Museum archivist in Camberley, England. The museum housed the archives of all the British support regiments, and the archivist had searched the RASC Journals for any references to an A.T. Maynard, with no success. He couldn't trace a soldier's unit via the serial number with the records they kept, he said, and suggested contacting the Public Records Office at Kew or the Historic Disclosures Unit at the British Army Personnel Centre, even though normally they only released the records to family members.

The Historic Disclosures Unit? Leave it to the British to have such an intriguing name for the bureaucratic arm of the British Army.

"Disclosures Unit," I wrote on a Post-it and stuck it on my computer screen, then logged off and went out to the backyard to try to fix the broken sprinkler. It took me a while to force off the rusted head, but I managed it. I was about to go back inside when I heard a plane flying low overhead. It looked like a vintage WWII plane, and it was following the mountain range in the direction of the Van Nuys airport to the north. The sound of its engines ebbed and flowed between the clouds, its open, half-moon cockpit framing the pilot's head, and I waved.

Back inside, I retrieved the Rhea file again. This time I didn't close it up right away. The first page contained a photocopy of six notes. They were tiny notes in Rhea's writing, all capital letters, written to my father, but as though three-year-old Dena had written them. Each one started with "dearest Daddy."

To my dearest Daddy, When can you come to see me? I miss you so very much. Don't you feel it? We ask you not to show any of these shots. You are not to share these pictures with <u>No One. Keep Them Hidden.</u>

Behind the photocopies of notes was a picture postcard from the Fontainebleau Hotel in Miami. It made me cringe, the pretty blueness of the sky, the aqua of the ocean. I couldn't look at the writing on the other side. I closed up the file, stuffed it back in my desk, and called my brother.

I was ten, and it was raining that day. We were on our way back from an outing in downtown Philadelphia and passed a house that looked like a castle out of a storybook. It had a red roof and towers with tops that looked like upside-down cones. Little flags sat above. "That's Maybrook Mansion," Aunt Ree pointed out to us. "Can you imagine the parties that rich dame gave there?" She sounded so sad.

When we got back to Aunt Ree's house, we took off our raincoats and played hide- and-seek, running up and down the staircase. Dena's older half brother, Leslie, was playing his record of West Side Story.

We had the run of the house for hide-and-seek, except for Aunt Ree's bedroom, which was strictly off-limits, but I couldn't find Dena, and Aunt Ree's bedroom door was ajar. I knocked on the door, and there was no answer. I knocked again and opened the door.

Inside, the room was dark, but I could smell the furs in her cedar closet, half-open, sucking the air out of the bedroom, and I could see the painting. It hung high above her four-poster bed. It was the handsome face of a man in three-quarter pose. His chin seemed soft, like the colors of the painting. I almost didn't recognize him.

It was my father.

Aunt Ree caught me standing near the painting.

I thought she'd be mad at me, but she wasn't. "You don't have to tell your mother. It's just our little secret, right, darling? Right, honey? Just a little, sweet secret between us."

I looked at the painting again, and then at Aunt Ree.

"It's okay. I won't tell." But I wondered. What made a secret sweet?

Nine

Oren's graduation came and went. From the balcony of Pauley Pavilion, I watched him and the hundreds of other graduates in caps and gowns march up the aisles to their seats, and it reminded me again of how fast time marched forward too with breakneck speed. At the end of the ceremonies, the graduates threw their caps up in the air, landing seconds later on the floor, and twenty-some years of Oren's infancy, childhood, teenage years, and new adulthood mashed up together in my head like a movie on fast-forward. Barely minutes ago, he was a blue-eyed towhead, taking tennis and guitar lessons and playing Little League baseball. Now he was over six feet tall. Getting up to leave and meet him down below, I was sure he hadn't seen us up among the hundreds of parents in the balcony, but just then I saw him turn around, smile, and wave up to us, and I saw the little boy again, the one who'd run through our house, jumping up in the hallway to tap the ceiling.

Throughout July, Bert continued to send me cheerful emails with helpful links for my research, but his correspondence started to segue mostly into funny stories about current events in Melbourne and his favorite activities, which included betting on horse racing and rugby championships, and playing lotto.

In early August, we were all invited to Ron's fortieth birthday dinner at a restaurant in Venice. My birthday was coming up a week later, but I wasn't looking forward to it. Every August ninth, TV reports reminded me that I was born exactly seven years after the last atom bomb of World War II fell on Nagasaki, Japan, and every year, the news would be full of remembrances of that day, old newsreel footage of the devastation the bomb, nicknamed "Fat Man," had wreaked on the city.

Before we left for the party, I checked my inbox, but as it had been for days, there were no new emails regarding Maynard. At the party, waiters with black aprons floated like messengers in and out of a private room with two long tables filled with guests, and for once my mother and father seemed animated. Just before dessert, Ron and his partner and future husband, Zach, came over to sit next to me. They'd been together for a few years now, enough time for my mother to set aside some of her constant worries for my brother—mostly about his safety in a world that had only just barely begun to accept gays. I worried for him too. There was still an atmosphere of job discrimination and attacks on gay couples, and same-sex marriage foes were ramping up their rhetoric this summer.

I was glad our parents had finally come to accept Ron's coming out, later attending Ron and Zach's commitment ceremony and supporting them in their hopes for same-sex marriage to be a reality one day.

Ron whispered in my ear, "It's been some time since you told me about that file, but you haven't said a word about it recently. Have you read it? Can you send it to me?"

"No, not yet." I looked at him. He was beginning to look more and more like our father.

"No? Really?" he said.

We were very different, my brother and I, and it wasn't just our ten-year age difference. My skin was more like my mother's, olive turning to tan. Ron had inherited my father's European baby-white paleness, burning easily in the sun. Ron too had somehow, and not biologically, inherited Rhea's can-do qualities. Even as a toddler, he'd been the family's chief debater and convincer, and while I stood back and looked out to achieve what I thought was possible, he was always aiming for what was seemingly out of reach. This quality, admirable as it was, was also sometimes exhausting, "no" being a response he didn't readily accept.

"Come on. It's your birthday. Let's not do this now. Did I ever tell you about the moment Mom told me I was going to have a sibling? It was so weird. She didn't actually tell me, but rather took me along with her to a local maternity store to try on some clothes. I remember there were all these smock-like dresses with giant bows and tentlike baby doll tops and I eventually guessed, but it seemed a strange way to tell me the news. I guess it was the beginning of me learning that I had to figure things out for myself," I said, laughing.

"Come on. You didn't even look at it?" he persisted.

I glanced at my mother standing and talking to one of Ron's friends. I hadn't seen her smiling in a long time. "Well, I did kind of look at just a couple of the notes."

Ron looked in the direction of my father sitting at the other table. "What did the notes say? You should really read all of it. And don't you think I should see them too?"

"Of course you should. And I'll tell you everything, show you everything, I promise, at some point soon."

∼

After the party, the rest of the summer was on fast-forward along with an increasing caseload. One morning in the judges' elevator, I briefly mentioned the postcard to Mark, a friendly colleague. He had a look of mild amusement.

"Aren't they keeping you busy enough down there in Juvenile Court?" he quipped.

"Yes, actually."

"Well, it sounds like fun, but I'd keep your little moonlighting *project* on the down-low and not share it with anyone else around here," he said, laughing as the door opened for his floor.

"Well—" was all I could manage to say before the elevator door closed, but his words rattled me. Whatever I was doing was on my own time, and no one's business. Little project? But what about the rumors I'd heard about the presiding judge and his frowning on "outside" activities? Two other judges had already been reassigned.

That afternoon I heard the trial of a girl cited for trespassing and drugs. She'd been arrested for breaking into a vacant house and using drugs. She admitted to both but explained that the older person arrested with her was her former boyfriend, who'd been abusive. He'd beat her up and once even cut off all her hair. Despite the restraining order she'd finally filed against him a year before, she'd felt lonely one night and met him at the vacant house. It was an easy case, with an admission at trial, and no need to excavate for the truth. But the girl's father had also abused her mother, several witnesses testified, a family pattern, the cycle of violence perpetuated by staying with an abuser.

"It's true she did it," her mother said. "But the truth isn't everything. There are many truths," the mother said and took her daughter's hand.

I was eleven, the only witness to the accident. I was the only one who saw the car that hit Dena while we were out riding our bikes. Aunt Ree came to tell my parents that I would have to go to court next Friday afternoon.

Everyone huddled in our tiny kitchen to talk.

Would I get back in time before the start of Shabbat? my grandfather worried. What if they asked me to swear on the Bible? my grandmother asked. I would have to speak up, my father insisted. I would have to say that I "affirmed" to tell the truth but not swear.

Speak up? I looked at the black tile behind the stove for an answer.

But I worried too about something else. What if the lawyer asked me if I had worn my glasses that day, which I hadn't?

I didn't want to go. I didn't want to go to court. I didn't want to affirm or swear to tell the truth, the whole truth, like they did on TV, or have to tell a judge I hadn't worn my glasses. Wasn't it good enough that I'd seen it and heard it all perfectly, the man speeding down the street, the sound of car tires, and Dena on the road, her bike and leg mangled? But it wasn't enough.

In the end, I didn't go. The judge had dismissed the case a day before the court date.

Ten

The next Sunday, it was drizzling, rare for Los Angeles in the summer, and the clouds seemed to make strange arcs across the sky, and the leaves of the lemon tree were wet with tiny droplets. I looked at my watch, and then got up and called my parents. I was sure they were out and wanted only to hear the outgoing message my father had recorded before the stroke that had affected his speech, and slowed it down.

But my mother answered the phone. "I knew it was you," she said instead of "Hello," her mom-telepathy on full throttle. "Is something wrong?"

"No, I just called to see how you're doing."

"Can't talk now, Leora. I'm on call waiting," she explained. "I'll call you back later."

I put the phone down and picked up a book about the British Army in World War II I'd found in the library. I'd put some more of the pieces of the postcard puzzle together by this time, learning about the Over-Seas League and its founder, Sir Evelyn Wrench, an author and politician who had also founded the English-Speaking Union. I'd even bought one of the original solicitation letters and response cards from the League on eBay, learning more.

The letter had come doubled over neatly into quarters, the paper ivory-colored, the fold itself worn and delicate. It was typewritten, very similar to the typeset on Maynard's postcard, and dated

November 27, 1942, ten days before Pearl Harbor. The letter had a grace to it, typed individually, as though it had gently been ushered into an envelope like egg whites into batter. There was a special feel to it, something that had made a long journey, different from the letters I usually printed out on my laser printer using cheap Office Depot brand multipurpose paper. There was an essence to the paper, an odor, unlike its virtual twin, the phantom email, and its ghost envelope.

The logo on the letter was a sailing ship atop an *O*, the *S* inside its globe. The name on the letterhead was the "Over-Seas League."

Twenty-five cents sends sixty Cigarettes, and a Reply Postcard ready-addressed to you. These are the Men Fighting for the Right to Be Free. Send Them Plenty of Smokes, a Tobacco Fund brochure pitched to prospective donors, but only British citizens or those of British "kinship" were invited to be prospective donors.

As a charitable organization, the league had held a US Department of State license, and I'd contacted the National Archives, which sent me copies of part of the file from 1941–1942. Portions of the file had been stamped "declassified," and they confirmed something I'd suspected—that the solicitation effort on the part of the League had been highly organized.

The list of Over-Seas League patrons on the back of the brochure read like characters from a nineteenth-century mystery novel. They included the Marquise of Ailsa, the Duchess of Atholl, the Archbishop of Canterbury, the Marchioness of Linlithgow, the Maharaja of Mysore, the Sultan of Zanzibar, and Earl Baldwin of Bewdley. I looked up all of their back stories, but Earl Baldwin of Bewdley's caught my eye.

Earl Oliver Baldwin had been a British politician, son of three-time Prime Minister Stanley Baldwin, and in August of 1931, the *Daily Mail* was dominated by a story claiming that Oliver Baldwin was secretly living with a man. The newspaper accounts sucked me in.

We do not know if Mr. Oliver Baldwin and Mr. Mark Boyle are indulging in unnatural vice, but if they are committing criminal acts, the police should be informed and a criminal prosecution brought.

Interesting, but Maynard's story remained a mystery. I hadn't even figured out his first name yet. Was it Albert like Bert from Australia? Or Arthur? Alan? Alex? I was going around in circles and falling into more and more rabbit holes that led nowhere. Who cared if Oliver Baldwin had lived with a man? Still, the solicitation pitch kept going round and round in my head.

These are men fighting for the right to be free.

It was still drizzling when Talia went to a practice, and David and I were in the car heading downtown for a concert, passing Hollywood. Just off the Cahuenga exit on the 101, the area was in the shadow of the Capitol Records building, which sat on a hill to mimic a stack of old records, its needle poking a hole into the skyline.

I turned to David. "I read somewhere that the light on the spire still flashed "Hollywood" in Morse Code, like an SOS." And in the darkening afternoon, Hollywood seemed submerged too, sinking in the rain. I caught a glimpse of the old Ivar Hills Apartments, on a street of buildings built in the 1920s before the roadway had been sliced in half by the Hollywood Freeway. "It's the apartment building where Nathaniel West wrote *Day of the Locust*, close to the Alto Nido Apartments where they'd filmed a scene from *Sunset Boulevard*. Oh, and look." I pointed. "There's a guy on a balcony jumping up and down."

David laughed. "You are your own information booth and news-room bulletin."

"Very funny." I grimaced.

"No. Cute, really."

"Sure." I laughed, and I took out the email I'd just received and printed out from Ruth, a member of the British Graphology Institute I'd found.

I felt really sorry for the man, she started. *It's good, as you indicated to me, that he probably survived the war, though I wonder how his life would have turned out after that.*

I turned to David. "Looks like you were right about the soldier being sad."

I read the rest of the email out loud to David.

Private Maynard was in quite poor shape physically, emotionally, and mentally, Ruth began, and I imagined the graphologist sitting in a drafty London house, speaking slowly and softly.

> *From the style of writing, no more than thirty, though the forms are exceptionally immature, even for a young man. His writing lacks the fluency that normally develops from the early teens, which suggests that he probably had the minimum of formal education and left school at fourteen or even earlier. Since this was usually due to economic necessity, it's likely that he came from a working-class or lower-middle-class background.*

It was something I'd guessed, but hadn't been sure. The postmark was from South Tottenham, a working-class area of North London, I'd discovered. Most maps of London didn't even include that part of the city, far from the usual tourist attractions, the palaces, parks, and galleries. I'd found the area only on a large scale map. Called Tottenham/Seven Sisters, the area had been named for the seven elm trees that grew in a circle by a roadside on Page Green, planted by seven sisters who were about to be separated.

> *He was warm and friendly, sentimental, with a school-boy's hand. Graphically, it shows a willingness to uphold the*

traditional values of the school system, such as conformity, obedience, cooperation, team spirit, industry, and productivity. Subjected to excessive discipline, his personal growth was stunted as he grew accustomed to concealing his emotions and maintaining the famous "stiff upper lip," and he gradually lost touch with his feelings.

Nevertheless, he had many qualities which would have suited him for army life. The hierarchical structure would have given him a sense of security and identity. He was loyal and could be relied on to do his duty. He was not a quick thinker, but he possessed sound common sense, and his actions were guided more by reason and instinct than emotion.

He respected authority, believed in fair play and sticking to the rules, and was capable of blind obedience to orders. He felt comfortable with strict routines because he knew what was expected of him, and he was afraid of making mistakes.

"That's pretty incredible she got all that from two sentences on an old postcard," David said.

"Pretty incredible, or a big stretch? But I wonder what she meant about him 'concealing his emotions'? You think he might be concealing something else? I read somewhere that putting more than one underline under one's signature meant that the person's self-worth was inadequate, a feeling of imperfection and incompleteness."

"Now that sounds like an even bigger stretch."

"Maybe it's all bunk? In court, handwriting analysis is sometimes not even admissible to authenticate a signature. So character analysis is probably just a bunch of junk science, right?"

"Who knows? Maybe not?" David said as we pulled into a downtown garage, and I folded up the email and put it behind me on the back seat.

Eleven

At the end of summer, the four of us flew to Kauai. Landing at the smaller airport, we were greeted by wild chickens roaming the tarmac and the scent of tropical flowers. As we drove through the million-year-old red clay fields and drizzly wetlands to our hotel, I took a deep breath. Both Oren and Talia were here with us, safe in our little island orbit. But I wondered, *Would it be the last vacation for the four of us?*

Later that first evening, Talia knocked on the door of our hotel room and announced, "Oren and I are going down to the lobby to hang out."

I looked at my watch. "But it's past eleven."

"We're on an island, remember? And this isn't Los Angeles, Mom," she said. "You don't have to worry here about us getting curfew tickets, like you always do."

"It's just that—"

"Come on, Mom. We're on vacation. And here no one knows us as *the* Juvenile Court judge's kids," she said.

I looked at David for help and he chimed in. "Okay, guys. Just don't come back too late." I knew they took a lot of ribbing from their friends because of my job. I knew that sometimes I'd been stricter with them because of it too.

"Yeah, okay."

I fell asleep and dreamt about my father, that he'd painted our old, Philadelphia house in bright colors, wild pinks and oranges. He then sat back on his desk chair, taking in the colors, and smiled, and I woke up thinking I couldn't remember the last time I saw my father smile that widely.

The next morning, David and I headed alone to the beach. It was good to get away from the phone, the internet, and the books I'd been reading about Britain and the Blitzkrieg. But World War II was here too. Out on the cliffs above the shore were huge concrete blocks dotting the coastline, remnants of WWII bunkers, painted green to blend into the landscape.

"Are we facing west?" David asked.

"Not sure." In California, west was where the sun would always set just above the ocean, but here on the island, my sense of direction was off. There was leeward and windward instead of north and south, east and west, the sun setting over mountains instead of the ocean, and for a moment I felt disoriented.

One afternoon, when the rest of the family went snorkeling, I couldn't resist stopping in at the hotel business center and found a response from the National Archives archivist about the rest of the Over-Seas Tobacco Fund file. There were 278 more Department of State pages relating to the fund, he wrote. I could order copies if I wanted. Almost three hundred pages of material? There had to be some answers there in that stack.

I immediately mailed him back and ordered the copies.

Later, I met up with David and the kids at the pool. David was talking to a little boy who had a tiny, green gecko sitting on his index finger.

"Where did you find the gecko?" David asked him.

"I didn't find him," the boy replied. "He found me."

"Just like Maynard, right?" David turned to me and laughed. "He found you."

On one of our last mornings, a local newspaper landed at our hotel door with news of the once-in-a-lifetime view of Mars over the next three nights. That night, the four of us went down to the ocean and rocked in hammocks by the beach, bathing in the trade winds and the light of the red planet.

Twelve

Talia went back to school after summer vacation. She passed her driver's test, and all weeklong afterward we bickered over stupid stuff, made up, then bickered again. Her new license meant I would lose that time I'd spent driving her around, and I was grieving for that precious time with her. I knew I wasn't doing a good job of making peace with her new independence, but I couldn't help myself. I should have remembered that for me, high school and a driver's license had also been a giant leap into my own autonomy, a chance to get away and discover who I was apart from my parents.

All September and October I shifted my focus, concentrating on W.H. Caldwell, the donor to whom the postcard was addressed. Maybe W.H. was the key to unlocking Maynard? I joined the New York Genealogical Society, searching online and ending up going off on a hundred tangents. But W.H. turned out to be easier to track down.

Over the Thanksgiving holiday, I called Maria, a genealogist I'd found who specialized in New York families, and spoke to her at length. Then I spent three days comparing the 1930 US Census online, which had no index for New York State, with the National Archive's list of enumerated districts. There, I unearthed some mistakes in the districting and finally found W.H. Caldwell on that and other US censuses, and then delved into his family history. I also came across a blogger whose grandfather once owned the Clinton Avenue apartment house and researched the shipping company

Caldwell's family had owned, along with his great-grandfather, who had been a sea captain.

I learned that W.H. stood for Watson Hallet, a foreign freight broker who was married and had lived at 275 Clinton Avenue in Brooklyn for years. In a 1907 newspaper advertisement, the apartment building was described as "high class and desirable in the finest section of Brooklyn," and included "hall boys and elevator service." Watson came from a well-known sailing and shipping family that could trace their lineage back to the first English settlers in Ipswich, Massachusetts. As someone with British "kinship," Watson was a perfect prospective donor for the Tobacco Fund solicitation campaign.

Childless, the couple was generous and made donations to many charitable causes. I also found society notices of their trips as passengers on the White Star Line to Europe and the Middle East and luncheons in the Pall Mall Room of the Ritz Carlton Hotel honoring the Grand Duke Boris of Russia in 1929.

It was all very interesting, but soon I was sure that spending time running down leads on Caldwell was taking me further and further away from finding Maynard again. Yet was there any connection to Maynard I wasn't seeing? I called Maria back and asked her to see if she could locate Caldwell's will in the public domain.

By December, six months after I'd found the postcard, I'd emailed a host of archivists and librarians, as well as dozens of random people I'd found on the internet, all with the subject heading "Inquiry." All my emails started out the same way.

Dear Ken.

Dear Mr. Livermore.

Dear Mr. Gustafson.

I was now fresh out of ideas. By now some of my correspondence had gone way beyond research. I'd exchanged family photos with octogenarian Bert from Australia, and made another newfound friend, Kay, someone who now lived in the same apartment building in Brooklyn as Caldwell. After sharing our personal stories, French-speaking Kay now began each email to me with *Ma Chère*, ending it with *Affectueusement*, and offered to post a letter on the building's bulletin board about Caldwell.

> *There are enough busybodies here who might be intrigued enough that they might engage in some sleuthing on your behalf. Voila!*

Remarkably, even most of the other people I contacted were also not only curious, but friendly and responsive, many cheering me on in my strange quest.

> *Good Luck.*
>
> *Cheers.*
>
> *Cheerio.*

One man I'd contacted in the UK even offered to write to his local member of Parliament.

> *MPs are obliged to reply to their constituents' questions and indeed obligated to help them where possible, so this may open some doors.*

I'd become a member of a number of genealogical societies, and registered with a host of organizations, collecting a long list of forgettable passwords and login names, even receiving "Dear Veteran" emails because I'd registered with so many veteran websites.

But everyone I'd contacted over the past few months for suggestions on how best to approach the British Army warned me it would be a waste of my time to write to them. World War II records were confidential, and they wouldn't release Maynard's service record to someone who wasn't a proven next of kin. I looked at the "Disclosures Unit" Post-it that was still half-stuck on my computer, and decided to ignore the advice.

I couldn't find an email address listed anywhere for the Historical Disclosures Unit of the British Army, only a mailing address at Kentigern House in Glasgow, so I wrote my first snail mail letter, making sure I emphasized that my intentions were honorable.

I only want to return the postcard to Private Maynard or his next of kin.

The next day, I drove to work early and walked over to the post office near the courthouse. There was a long line of people waiting, some resting their packages on the thin counter that ran across the length of the area. Quiet, the only sound was that of the automatic doors shushing open and closed, and I looked around. Post offices no longer merely sold postage as they did when Maynard had bought his two red stamps in South Tottenham. They now sold phone cards and stuffed bears, *Dear Santa* CDs and wrapping paper. But Maynard too must have stood in a similar line, waiting for the postal clerk to call out for another patron, and I could feel his presence, his footfall each time I took a step forward.

I tried to imagine what the post office in South Tottenham would have looked like in the early forties. It would have been smaller than this half-block-long building in Van Nuys, with its large plate glass windows and blinds and the linoleum floor. Last week, I'd contacted the Royal Mail to see if they had a list of post offices in South Tottenham in 1942, but their research advisor wrote me back saying the list of post offices in London had stopped being compiled in 1937. Currently, there were three South Tottenham, N15, post offices, and I couldn't decipher whether any of the three had been open in 1942.

I thought about the small insight into Maynard when I'd read one of the Over-Seas League solicitation brochures explaining mailing procedures.

Since at present a solider has to pay postage on correspondence to the USA, donors will understand the reason if a Reply Postcard is not received in every case.

Maynard could have easily taken his parcel of cigarettes and not responded to his American donor. Instead, he'd purchased his own stamps to thank Caldwell. The soldier had gone out of his way.

When I reached the head of the line, the clerk told me I needed an eighty-cent airmail stamp, and produced one with the bluish image of snow-capped Mount McKinley. I bought the stamp and then asked for fifty more. I'd probably be writing more letters, I figured.

The next day, I needed a new eye, and I removed the postcard from the little fire safe in my office where I now kept it, took it to the nearest Kinko's, and had both sides enlarged. The two-by-four card morphed into eight-by-eleven, taking up a full page. By multiplying the area by 1,100 percent, the tiny postcard found a new proportion, Maynard's words almost jumping off the page. I looked at the piles of papers on my desk. One pile contained all the emails I'd received from Bert in Australia. They were smart and funny, full of wild wallpapers and colorful animations, as Bert continued to send me new resource materials and links. But in one email, he described his childhood home in New Malden, a suburb of London, and the German bombing of August 1940.

My mother used her best tablecloth to help bandage a casualty
lying in the road outside our house, and afterwards found a
shilling there. Must have been her destiny, don't you think?

Again, I was nowhere closer to finding Maynard. Where was "destiny" in all this? I crumpled up all the papers on my desk and threw them into the trash basket. Then I went back to the trash basket, gathered up what I'd thrown away, and uncrumpled them.

A few weeks later, I was about to leave the house when the mailman drove up. In the jumble of bills and catalogs was the polite form letter I'd expected from the Army Personnel Centre, Historical Disclosures. Large, the envelope was distinct, thin, the color of ash wood, different from the manila envelopes used in the US. It was from Bernadette P. Hand, Administrative Officer, but it surprised me. She mentioned nothing about confidentiality in her letter.

Unfortunately, army records are not very helpful in tracing
the whereabouts of someone who left the army many years
ago.

I read the letter twice, then threw it on the kitchen table. I made a mental list of all the avenues I'd taken—the British tracing service, letters to archivists and librarians in the north of London, the myriad of veterans organizations, all with no result. I'd contacted "Service Pals," which screened requests for locating military people twenty-four hours a day for seven consecutive days, often fielding fifty or sixty requests a day. I queried every RASC veteran I could find on the internet, and on top of that, the 278 pages from the Department of State I'd ordered had been useless, just a bunch of inquiries to the Department of State asking if the Tobacco Fund was legitimate. My internet searches were going nowhere as well.

Your search did not match any documents.

Sorry, your search did not return any hits.

The criteria you have entered have not provided any results.

Forbidden: You don't have permission to access the content on this server.

I'd even started writing letters to random Maynards in London.

Maybe you will just have to make your Maynard up, Kay wrote me from Brooklyn.

"Maybe it's time to give this whole thing up?" I complained to David when he came home from work. "I'll probably never find him. I should give up."

"Really?" he said, getting a drink from the refrigerator. "Do you really have to go there?"

"But that's me. I go there."

Suddenly I thought about Rhea. What would she have said about that? Would she have given up?

I went to my office, pulled out the Rhea file, and brought it into the kitchen to show David. "Look at this." It was a cryptic note about some gift packages that had been sent from Florida to my grandmother and father, and a package for my mother.

> *This was gotten for Yael. But we thought she could use the other thing better. You can keep this for yourself as a gift at some other time. We don't want you to share the pictures or their meaning with NO ONE.*

"A package for my mother too? Chutzpa, right?"

"Yep, pretty cheeky."

"But that's Rhea," my father used to say, shaking his head every time she did something like that, came up with some impossible-sounding scheme, or announced some last-minute, middle-of-the-night drive to a far-off city. But it was more than her persistence and audacity—it was some sort of inborn, wild optimism that anything was possible, a concept so foreign but so seductive to me in my parents' house of postwar fatalism and gloomy cynicism, where you're always waiting for some shit to hit the fan.

"You'll figure it out," he said. "I know you will."

"Sure, sure," I said, still skeptical.

I went back to my office and picked up the letter from the British Army disclosure unit and looked at it again.

I must have missed it the first time. The typeface was almost microscopic, and it sat like another one of Rhea's unconventional "gifts" in the upper right corner of the letter—an email address for Bernadette Hand, the British Army signatory, an email address I'd never come across in any of the materials about the Historical Disclosure Unit. I immediately emailed her, made a copy of my email, and scrawled "One Last Try" across my copy.

I typed in quickly, about to click "Send" when my eye caught the formatting boxes above my email—bold, italic, underline.

I highlighted the word "disclose," pressed "underline," and sent it off.

I understand you cannot <u>disclose</u> the record, but could you please confirm A.T. Maynard's first and second name?

One afternoon, Aunt Ree took Dena and me along with her to Fort Dix to see her cousin who was an army dentist. I liked the long ride in the back of her car to New Jersey, and stopping at Howard Johnson's for an ice cream sundae. At the army base, a handsome soldier raised the gate to let us in. He smiled and waved to me as we passed by, and I smiled back.

On our way home, Aunt Ree stopped at a store and bought me my first bra. "It's my gift. But just put it away somewhere," she said with a wink. It was barely a bra, a size AAA confection of lace, but it was mine, and I loved her for that and all the other gifts that appeared like magic—bicycles and Barbies, ballerina lamps and giant teddy bears. Cinderella had a fairy godmother. But I had Aunt Ree.

When I got home, I didn't do a good job of hiding it, and my mother found it in my dresser drawer. She took it and threw it up onto the top shelf of our hall closet. "You're too young for that," my mother insisted.

"But it's mine."

"She shouldn't have done that. She's not your mother."

Later that summer, Aunt Ree landed impossible-to-get seventh row tickets to the Beatles concert at the convention center for Dena and me. My mother didn't want me to go, but somehow she was outvoted.

The night before the concert, I snuck down to the hall closet and pulled out the bra. And at that concert, even in the chaos of music and thirteen thousand screaming, and underneath the little girl blouse my mother picked out for me, I could feel it. It was mine, the soft edges of an AAA bra.

Thirteen

I was the last month of 2003, and one Saturday morning, I volunteered to finalize foster parent adoptions at the Children's Court in Monterey Park, one of the few—possibly the only—"happy" assignments in the entire court system. Instead of worried parents and teens and combative lawyers, the courtroom was a place of smiling new families, balloons, and stuffed animals. It was the only time cameras and a photo with me, as judge, was allowed for three short but heartwarming hours. "A place where what was once broken could now be fixed," one of the clerks commented to me, and I left feeling a new hopefulness.

The next day, Talia left for Cabo, Mexico, with a friend and her friend's parents on a small plane. David and I drove her to the local Van Nuys airport, completely surprised we were allowed to drive right up to the jet. The captain smiled down at us from the airplane door, but my heart skipped a beat as I watched her walking up the four foldaway steps into the ten-seater plane.

"Call me as soon as you get there," I yelled up to her, the noise on the tarmac almost deafening.

"I will," Talia yelled back.

"Don't forget," I yelled out once more, and the door closed, and we watched the plane take off to the south.

Oren was also leaving in a few days for his trip to South Africa. He'd moved back in after graduation for a few months, but was now looking for an apartment to share with friends. I came home and wrote an email to my friend and writing buddy, ex-Utahan Carolyn. "Next week will be my first double empty nest," I complained.

Carolyn, always as practical as her deep Salt Lake City roots, set me straight. "How many of us get a chance to go anywhere on a private jet? You did good by letting her go and be independent."

That same week, my father failed to pass his driver's license test. His loss of independence and his reliance on my mother to drive him around made him even quieter than before, and it seemed as though he was closing another chapter in his life.

The last months of WWII had been the setting of one of those chapters. Knowing that Germany would be defeated, Romania switched sides, suspending deportation of Jews and permitting limited emigration to Palestine. Small groups of Jews were allowed to leave Romania, and leaving his parents behind, my father fled on land via Constantinople and Syria, and finally by sea on the *Maritza*, a Bulgarian fishing boat deemed unseaworthy by the Red Cross and which, on another sailing, sank in a storm. When he landed in the British Mandate of Palestine, he was detained for being an illegal immigrant at the British Atlit Detention Camp, where refugees from the Holocaust were housed in barracks surrounded by barbed wire and guard towers.

After being released with nowhere to stay, he slept on a Tel Aviv park bench and survived on the unsellable pieces of broken chocolate brought to him by a distant cousin who worked at a chocolate factory. Two years later, he left Palestine and returned to postwar Europe, to the Prague Music Conservatory, to study music and participate in an international music contest in which he won second prize. On his return to Palestine, he joined the Haganah and the fledgling Israel Opera, founded by American soprano Edis de Philippe. There, in a rehearsal for *Fra Diavolo*, a comic opera by French composer Daniel Auber, where he played the innkeeper Matheo, he met my mother, Yael, who was in the chorus.

~

I came along with them the first time my mother drove him to his favorite pastime—the sauna.

"How are you?" she asked, as we sat down to wait for him at a nearby Starbucks overlooking busy Olympic Boulevard. Then, over cappuccinos, she related a *Judge Judy* episode she'd watched on television that morning. My mother couldn't get enough of Judy Sheindlin, admiring her tough-as-nails wit and her keen talent for detecting lies. "She doesn't take any BS from anybody."

"Yeah, she's great," I said. "But you do know that I couldn't do what she does or says in her TV courtroom."

"Yes, yes, I know that," she sighed. "But it's a shame you can't."

I laughed. Over the years at court, I'd also developed a strong inner bullshit meter, an aversion to lies and half-truths, but maybe it was also because of the DNA my uber-detective mother had passed along to me.

After Starbucks, we went back into her car near the sauna. It was cold outside, the car windows were up and the car felt like a warm womb. It was as good as any time to tell her.

"You know that postcard I told you about a few months ago," I began, and told her about the last few months of my search for Maynard. She paused for a moment.

"I think it's a great project for you."

Again that word, *project*. "It's not a *project*," I bristled.

"I didn't mean anything, Leora, I just—"

"It's okay," I interrupted her. "I know you think it's stupid, a waste of my time. And money, right?"

"No. Not at all. Not at all. But I think you better check and see whether you need to renew your passport," she suddenly said.

"How did you know I was thinking about—"

"I didn't, but I know you. But maybe it's still a bit too early to book a flight?" she asked.

"Maybe, but I have to do something."

"Sometimes, there's nothing you can do. And from what you said, you haven't even found him yet. You don't even know if he's alive."

"I know that," I said, and I looked out the window to the house across the sidewalk. It had probably been a simple ranch-style house when it was built, but someone had added columns and intricate moldings above the door.

"I want to show you something quickly before *he* comes back." She turned to the back seat to retrieve her handbag, then pulled something out of it.

"See this?" She pointed to some jewelry that was wrapped in a handkerchief. "He won't get rid of it. I begged him to give it away or sell it, but he won't do it."

"What are you talking about?"

"The jewelry, the jewelry *she* gave him. You won't believe it. You won't believe what I found. I knew she'd given him jewelry, but I didn't know they all have writing inside. Secret writing," she sputtered.

My mother handed me the handkerchief and I opened it up. There were two large cuff links and a tie clip. She showed me how the cuff links opened to reveal engravings. On one side, two hearts with my initial intertwined with Dena's. Inside the other cuff link, two more hearts with my father's *L* initial and Rhea's *R*, Rhea's heart broken in half, and a date—April 22, 1958. Alongside the date, the inscription "my biggest heartache." There was also a ring that opened up and a few other diamond trinkets.

I looked across the seat and saw my mother's sea-green eyes behind her glasses.

"You see now? You understand me, now? A broken heart?" she huffed. "What about my heart?"

I reached out to touch her hand. It was soft, so soft, not even one callus, like baby skin, like it had always been, and I didn't want to let go. But the softness didn't match the sadness mixed with anger in her voice. "I know," I said.

"Why won't he let it go and get rid of it, sell it or give it away? Why does he keep these things?"

I thought about the file, the fact that he'd kept that too. "I don't know, Mom."

"I thought he was my best friend. We were both so poor when we first started going out together that when we went together to a café, we couldn't even order two coffees. We had to share one glass of soda water. But we were happy."

Meeting my father while singing in the chorus of the Israel Opera's production of *Fra Diavolo* had been the happy turning point in my mother's early life. She was six years younger than he, but when she saw the handsome, wavy-haired European with a very un-Sabra bow tie at the first rehearsal, it was love at first sight. She immediately told herself she was going to marry him.

Although she had to promise him to keep kosher and keep the Shabbat, something she'd never done before, she willingly took it on herself, and their life after Israel's War of Independence was relatively happy. My mother worked as an assistant to the head of the newly formed Shin Bet, Isser Harel, who later became best known for pursuing and capturing Nazi Adolf Eichmann in Argentina. She worked for Harel in a secret location until she was eight months pregnant with me. My father had a government job with the Tnu'at Hamoshavim, the labor movement's department of culture. His parents emigrated from Romania to Israel three months after my parents were married. The government allotted my parents an apartment on the outskirts of Tel Aviv, and I was born there.

She took the handkerchief and jewelry from my lap and shoved it back in her purse.

"When he went to America first, I thought it was for us, that it would be good for us, for our new little family, for you and me. I was so naive. When my neighbor said to me, 'You don't let a young man go so far away like that without you,' I thought that nothing could happen. Boy, was I wrong! When I landed with you in New York, and saw *her* there at the airport with him, I knew it. I knew something was wrong. I knew it, but he denied it and denied it, and I didn't do anything about it. And as much as I'm mad at him, I'm mad at myself, and that's the truth of it."

"She was there at the airport when we landed?"

This was a version of our landing in the States that I'd never heard before. She'd never mentioned that Rhea had been there when we arrived, only the funny anecdote that when I first saw my father after almost a year of him being away, I, at two and a half years old, didn't recognize him. And when he'd reached out to me and told me that he was my father, I responded with "No, my father is in America."

I looked out again at the house through the car window. The columns looked ridiculous, silly beneath the ranch's wood-shingled roof. Still, wasn't reinvention and redemption, even silly, the birthright of homeowners in the City of Angels, a city known for its wild cocktail of building styles and neighborhoods? Ahead, toward the west, this part of the city stretched thin and low, and a foamy sky sat atop the porous landscape.

I took my mother's hand again and held it in mine.

"I do understand how you feel," I said. "What can I say to make you feel better? What can I do?"

She shook her head. "You can't," she said, and we sat there like that for a while until my father came back into the car.

On the drive back to their house, no one spoke.

Just a couple of weeks earlier at Children's Court, I'd been able to fix something, finalize an adoption, and make a family whole. And even in my usual courtroom, I could find and compel solutions to issues, empowered by law to impose compromises on warring parties. It was what I liked best about being a judge. But I had no power or authority here, no jurisdiction, no clerk or bailiff, no magic in the state seal above me. I couldn't repair what had been broken between my parents.

I rolled my window all the way down and took in the cool Los Angeles air. Maybe there was something else I could do. Maybe I could take the gifts Los Angeles had given me—its forgiving nature, a place where redefinition was the norm—and use them to give comfort somewhere else, to someone else. Maybe I could make some other gesture of redemption. And in the car, in the quiet between my mother and father, and in the silence and the racket of the jewelry buried in my mother's purse, I decided. I would go to London, no matter what.

We were on our way to my mother's music academy, and in the car, she hummed to herself as the wind whistled with her through the partly open window. Inside the academy and just off the staircase, there was a central hall of arches, and glass doors opened into wood-paneled music rooms. I sat beneath the long-legged grand pianos, listening to the sounds of the ticking metronomes.

The nice cook came to take me down to the basement kitchen with her and gave me alphabet soup. I lost my way back up the narrow stairway. But then my mother's voice came down the steps to guide me back. I could hear it spilling over with promises of concert halls and glossy programs, rows of faces in dimming houselights.

She was the beautiful widow Norina in Don Pasquale today, a comic opera, she explained when I found her. But there was also scheming, a mock marriage, and a veiled false bride.

So anch'io la virtù magica,

"I also know the magic virtue of a glance at the right time in the right place. I also know how hearts burn on the slow fire of a short smile."

Later in the afternoon, she leaned over an accompanist in another room, and his fingers flew up and down the keys until he hit one bad note. He hit the key again and again and still it made a sour sound. "Looks like this piano needs to be tuned," the accompanist declared. I heard it too, the off sound it made, like the bleat of a sheep.

"Tuned?" I asked, worrying what he meant.

"It just means that it needs to be fixed," he said.

"Oh, fixed." It sounded like a good thing.

Fourteen

Later that night, I couldn't sleep. At three in the morning, the house was quiet, and I got up and went online. I visited the American Airlines and British Airways sites first, but Virgin Atlantic seemed a strangely more appropriate choice with its bold, red-splashed website, and I started filling in departure and return dates.

Number of passengers?

One, I typed in. No. I didn't want to go alone, and David would be busy at work. *Two*. I would take Talia along with me, I decided. It would be a mother-daughter trip, our first. But when? June, six months from now, I decided. June would mark a year since I'd found the postcard.

Continue, the page encouraged, after I typed in my name, address, and phone number, but I jumped at the sound of the refrigerator motor suddenly turning on in the kitchen, and I missed filling in one of the questions.

Please recheck fields marked with an asterisk, the page gently scolded me, and then again, this time when I incorrectly entered the area code of my phone number.

Continue.

I chose the departure and returning flights and our seats from the seat planner link, then stopped just as I was about to fill in my credit card number. I dragged the mouse in circles on the pad.

This was crazy.

Each step of the booking has a limit of ten minutes, the page warned me, but I sat frozen in my chair. I couldn't click on the next *Continue* button, watching the tiny digital clock on the bottom right-hand side of the computer ticking away the minutes. I clicked on the *Back* button instead.

A ghost-white admonition appeared at the top of the screen.

Warning: Page Has Expired.

I couldn't return to the page I was on and was redirected back to the original home page. I'd have to start the booking process all over again from the beginning, and wondered whether the warning was meant for me. It was already quarter to four, and I knew I would have to wake up and go to work in a couple of hours. I could make the reservation later in the morning, I decided, and was about to log off when Talia slipped into the room.

"What are you doing up so late, Mom?"

"I'm trying to buy airline tickets to London."

"You're going to London?" she said, yawning.

"We're going."

"We? You mean you and I? Really? Tell me everything in the morning," she said with another yawn. "Aren't you going to bed?"

"Soon," I said, and I returned to the Virgin Atlantic site, filling in the fields again, retyping the data. Finally, I scrolled down to the last command.

Confirm.

And I did, printing out the three-page e-ticket.

An hour later, I was still on the internet, taking virtual tours of London apartments. Almost dizzy, I followed the arc of the 360-degree camera and looked at flats in Mayfair and Chelsea, Soho and Notting Hill. After a while, the apartments all looked the same— chintz living rooms and compact kitchens, white-tiled bathrooms and spare bedrooms. Finally, I settled on an apartment on Chesham Place, mostly for the soft sound of its name, the small private park that intersected the street, and the light that seemed to insinuate itself through the windows.

Fifteen

The next morning I was on my computer again when I heard Talia call out. "Come on, Mom. We're going to be late."

"Coming."

Talia's dance team had signed up for a series of competitions all over Southern California, and today's competition was at Loyola Marymount University.

"Mom?"

"Just a minute."

I'd just received an email from Maria, the New York genealogist. She'd tracked down the last will and testament of Watson in the records room of the Surrogate's Court, King's County, New York, and she'd attached copies for me. I clicked on the attachment, skimming over it quickly. There were bequests to cousins and other family members, and then a long list of donations to various charitable organizations—the YMCA, the Faith Home for Incurables, the Society for the Prevention of Cruelty to Children, the Home for the Blind, and a couple of local churches.

"Mom, come on."

"Okay," I called out to her, but the last paragraph caught my eye—a bequest to an "A.M.," care of a New York bank. Who was A.M.? But I had no time now to dig further. I would have to read the rest after Talia's competition.

"I'm coming."

"Can you please get off that computer and stop that *research* of yours for now?" Talia appeared at my door, her team bag thrown across her shoulder. "I can't be late," she said, and her bag fell with a thud on the floor.

"Sorry," I said, reaching out to touch the ends of her hair, but she took a step back.

"I know all this stuff's important to *you*, but it's annoying when you always have your head glued to that screen.

"I'm sorry," I repeated, logging off. "I know I kind of lose track of time."

"Yeah, I noticed," she said, pouting.

But in the car, I reached out to touch the ends of her hair again, and this time she didn't pull away. I looked at my watch. "We really do actually have plenty of time, even enough time for a quick bite somewhere," I said, and on the way I pulled into a McDonald's.

Inside the restaurant, I picked up a french fry, smothered it in ketchup, and wolfed it down. "Don't you just love these fries?"

"They're okay, I guess," Talia said.

"Oh, come on. Just okay? Rhea used to take Dena and me to McDonald's on the way back from school sometimes," I said. "But she always made sure to tell my father when we came back that we only ate filet of fish and fries so that he wouldn't think that we might have eaten some unkosher burger there." I laughed. "And she always complained that the milk wasn't cold enough. She only drank ice-cold milk, but it was always a big treat to go there."

"McDonald's, a big treat? Really?" Talia laughed.

"Yeah, for me it was. When I was growing up, we never went out to eat in restaurants together as a family. All our meals were cooked by my grandmother and eaten at home. Those fast-food stopovers with Rhea made me feel like I was a real American girl, like the girls on TV."

"Wow. I get that now," she said, as I looked at the last french fry on the tray. "Go ahead, Mom, you have it," she said, laughing, and pushed the tray closer to me.

When we were done, we got back into the car, and I drove southwest to the college perched on a mesa overlooking the lowlands of Playa Del Rey. The campus was a crisscross of straight lines, wide, open spaces of grass and buildings, palms planted in rows to tame the Jesuit landscape. Out to the west was the stormy Pacific. Down below in the wetlands there were still the traces of saltwater and freshwater marshes, bordered by the Ballona Creek, where the Los Angeles River had shifted over time, leaving a lagoon in its wake.

It started to rain just as we got to the gymnasium for the Spirit Association meet, and inside, the rain was pounding against the roof. I sat in the second tier, and the wooden floor seemed to help catapult each team's music up into the high ceiling. Even the banners hanging neatly from railings couldn't absorb the sounds, which also competed with the crowd of parents talking in the stands.

Soon, Talia's team entered the gymnasium and came out to the dance floor. Positioning themselves in the middle, they waited for their music to begin, and when it did, I watched Talia pass her hand above her head as her feet took hold of the floor. She was interpreting the music, decoding and breaking down the movement and music in her own way, translating it into motion, and I was happy dance had given her this.

I continued to watch the team's routine, arms and legs in unison. As they danced, I closed my eyes. Outside the gym, the rain came down harder now, pounding the roof, as though someone was knocking on a closed door.

My mother took music with her everywhere she went. It even drifted with the flapping laundry she hung out to dry in the morning. I followed her to the breezes of our backyard and held out the box of wooden laundry pegs, handing them to her one at a time. She bent over the plastic basket of wet clothes, singing. Then she plucked them up and pinned each wrung-out mass on the clothesline like notes on sheet music.

"We bend and clip, like violin bows, rising and falling," she said, laughing.

I couldn't wait to get back into the house and write it all down—the breeze and the feel of the wet clothes, the sound of my mother's voice. Writing it down, I could leave something behind. The words could live after me. And I had to do it. I had to leave something behind too, like her, like the girl in the diary, like Anne Frank.

Later in the afternoon, we came out again to the backyard to gather up the dry, stiffened bedsheets just before the rainstorm hit. We each held two corners outstretched. Then walked toward each other, folding and refolding, until the palms of our hands met.

"Presto, presto," she said, quick, quick, as the first droplets fell. "The rain is knocking on our door," she said, laughing. And we rushed to pull the rest off the line, but the rain met us halfway to the house.

Sixteen

Back home from the competition, I read over Watson's will, this time carefully. All the bequests to family and charities were specific, and included full names and relationships along with addresses. Only that one bequest stood out.

> *Article VI: All the rest, residue and remainder of my estate, of whatsoever kind and nature, and wheresoever situate, I give, devise and bequeath . . . ten shares to A.M., c/o Central Hanover Bank and Trust Company, of the City of New York.*

Could the mysterious "A.M." possibly be my A.T. Maynard or just some wishful thinking on my part?

The next Sunday, I drove up to see Carolyn, her house tucked away in the shadow of the Glendale hills. Just off the freeway, the road to her house morphed from an upscale housing tract of Spanish-style homes into a mountain road through hills of brush and scrub and large electrical towers, then back again into another housing tract. When I reached her house, I smelled sweet lavender as I walked up the driveway, and her four-foot-tall great Dane, Trixie, greeted me at the door.

Inside, Carolyn made a pot of tea from some of the herbs in her garden, and we settled down to talk about kids, movies, and writing. I'd been to her house many times before, but today I suddenly noticed the collection of vintage typewriters in her living room. I got up to look at the compact, gray-green Underwood, and pressed on a couple of the old keys.

"These are kind of like the typewriters—" I started.

"They used in the early forties. Yes, like on your postcard," Carolyn finished my thought. I'd already shared with her most of my research and late-night misgivings about the postcard, keeping her in the loop about my lack of progress. But Carolyn, always optimistic, wasn't fazed. Her writer's brain had already imagined dozens of scenarios, endings, and possibilities for me. "Don't give up now. I can already see you as describing him on the battlefield, bravely delivering his supplies," she said. "Why don't you take one of these home with you and feel it out?" Carolyn asked.

"What? A typewriter?"

"Yeah," she said, her sky-blue eyes sparkling. "Come on. Who knows, maybe it will speak to you." Carolyn laughed and poured me another cup of tea.

"Sounds like a bit of voodoo," I said.

"Oh, c'mon," Carolyn insisted. "What could it hurt?" And I ended up bringing the typewriter home with me.

At home, I set it down on my kitchen table. The top was dusty but alive with the swing of the carriage return, its click and ring, the black roller, the keys jumping up in a half circle. A quick search of the serial number on the internet revealed that it had been manufactured in the early forties, just about the time the solicitation letters were typed up by the volunteers at the Over-Seas League. I remembered seeing the pages and pages of donors and those who had agreed to collect money for the fund in the file sent to me by the National Archives in Washington, DC, and I wondered how many hours it had taken some overworked secretary to type out all the letters on cumbersome typewriters like this.

I tried out a couple of letters, but the black ribbon was completely worn out, unusable. I went online and bought a ribbon on eBay, and the ribbon came a few days later in a small, square box, a Black Hawk brand that looked like it had been forgotten and dug out of someone's old desk. But the spool and cloth ribbon inside were completely new and wrapped in cellophane.

When I opened the package, my fingertips became messy with ink, messier still when I placed the new spool on one of the typewriter's spindles and wound it up. I wiped them clean, typed out "W.H. Caldwell," then tapped out Caldwell's Brooklyn address. The keys had to be struck hard. They were round, with a distinct rim, like tiny, old-fashioned spectacles. Each letter clattered downward and commandeered its own individual amount of ink from the ribbon, none uniform. Some letters were top heavy with ink, fading at their ends, others not. The periods poked a tiny hole through the paper, perforating it. But the letters looked almost exactly the same as the typeface on the postcard, and it made me wonder. There must have been some reason the postcard had survived all these years. Why would Caldwell have even kept such a thing and not thrown it into his Clinton Avenue apartment trash to be churned up by the Brooklyn city dump if it hadn't meant something to him?

All those initials kept swirling around in my head—A.T., W.H., and now A.M. too.

A.T., W.H., A.M., I typed out, then random words and phrases. Suddenly "still waters" came to mind.

Still waters.

We were late. My mother took my hand, and we ran past a garden wall of stone and hurried to the outdoor pavilion where the opera was being staged. An hour before, I'd watched her put on her dress and brush on the powdery, green eye shadow that matched her eyes.

Soon, I was sitting in the audience with my new black patent leather shoes. It was a night of summer and shadows, the smell of flowers, the pink of my mother's cheek, turning marble in the spotlight. A pretty silk rippled and stretched across the stage, imitating water, and she rose from the pond to meet her prince. She seemed to walk on the water and float through the air, her saddest errand to meet her prince and watch him die. She wore the iridescent blue of Rusalka, the tragic nymph in the opera of the same name. The costume was perfect, a symphony of layers, a gauzy chiffon. Almost transparent, it fluttered and rested with her every movement.

"Brava, brava!" the audience yelled out, and my mother bowed. But the next morning, she sat in my father's office typing out a speech for him. "He leads me beside still waters," she typed, a phrase he often used from the twenty-third Psalm. "Aren't you done yet?" my father asked, standing over her and tapping his foot. She gave him an annoyed look. "No, not yet," she said, and she twisted the carriage and lifted the paper out just a bit so she could pinpoint the misspelling. She brushed on a correcting fluid, blew on it gently to dry, retyped the word, and pulled the paper out of the carriage, handing it to my father. But then she turned to me and sighed. "When you type too well, you stay a typist. Don't be like me," she said.

Seventeen

Dear Leora: I am not *British Army Private A.T. Maynard. Sorry I cannot help you. Yours Sincerely, Alan Maynard.*

It was a couple of days after New Year's when I received the first response to the ten letters I'd sent to random North London Maynards I'd found on 192.com, a British online telephone directory. Normally, I'd have been discouraged and thought of it as another setback, but I was weirdly optimistic. The word *not* felt like a typo. After all, there was only one small word in that sentence that needed to be omitted, I told myself, only a tiny adjustment, a correction.

Besides, I was also excited to try out the new laptop I'd gifted myself, charging it up on the kitchen counter. Then I went on my old PC and checked out all the Wi-Fi hot spots in the valley, noting some of them down. From now on I wouldn't be tied to the desktop computer in my house. I could take the internet with me wherever I went.

The beginning of January was unseasonably warm. Talia was at a friend's house, I was still off from work, and I invited my mother to take a ride over to Paradise Cove off Pacific Coast highway. As we drove, every building on the way to the beach looked like a mirror, the tinge of blue of a bird's egg. After we arrived and parked, we walked past a restaurant, toward the bluff, stretching out on a blanket beneath its shadow. I took out the laptop and tested out the UK–Info Disk "People Finder" I'd ordered. The disk was advertised to contain sixty-three million records compiled from three UK databases: the 2002 electoral roll, the 2003 electoral roll, and residential and business telephone listings. It prompted me to enter a surname, and all matching results would be returned.

"So, have you found your Maynard yet?" my mother asked me. For a while now, my mother had started to refer to the private as "your Maynard," as though he belonged to me.

"Stop calling him that. He's not mine."

"But have you found him?"

"Not yet. But I'm still trying." I told her about the tracing service I'd found through the Forces Reunited website, called 1st Locate. They'd written me that they'd completed the "normal searches" over a twenty-eight-day period and had not been able to trace A.T. Maynard. But they'd passed my request on to someone experienced in genealogical matters and were attempting to establish new leads.

"What about this CD you brought along?"

"I'm not sure it'll help," I replied, as I inserted the disk into my new laptop and plugged in the information. "It looks like there are two possible A.T. Maynards. One is Andrew T. Maynard from the 2002 electoral roll, the other, an Andrew T.W. Maynard from the 2003 electoral roll. The first has an address in Pembroke Dock, in Wales, and the other in Portsmouth."

"You see, I've brought you good luck," she said, fluttering.

"I guess you have."

"Can I see?" she asked, and she reached out to touch the laptop.

I handed it to her and looked around. Only part of the old, white-washed pier remained, much of it destroyed by the El Niño storms of the 1980s. Still, the pier's pilings interlaced gracefully into the Pacific Ocean, the water darkening the timber.

"I can't believe the information that's out there now about people," she said, returning the laptop to me. "Too much, don't you think? There are some things better left buried."

"You should get DSL for your computer, Mom. You're missing so much."

"I'd rather just call and hear someone's voice, instead of all this email business. People are stuck to a screen instead of being out in the world," she said.

"You and I are different, Mom. I love the new technology. Without the internet, I'm sure I wouldn't have any chance of finding Maynard. It's amazing," I said, defending the net as though it was a newly introduced boyfriend.

But she was partly right. There were already phishing expeditions from fake banks and credit unions, PayPal, and eBay accounts. So too, the websites I'd visited had left a trail of cookies, spawning fresh mutations—Viagra and human growth hormone offers, Russian brides, Ethiopian princes, and Nigerian colonels who showed up in my inbox despite spam filters. This new crop of bulk email was full of "find anyone" come-ons, luring amateur detectives and prying neighbors. "*The truth is out there . . . about everyone you know. No Secrets*," one site implored. "*Internet Spy Is Here—Find Out Anything about Anybody.*" "*Need to Find Something Out?*" asked another.

Delete, delete, delete, I'd press over and over, and what was once a time-saver was also starting to rob me of precious minutes.

"Okay, I see your point. Even some of the legit websites I've visited can be so time-consuming. I don't know how many sites I've registered with, each one asking for a user name and password, some insisting on different combinations of letters and numbers, some case sensitive, others not. I've got so many passwords and PINs now."

"Can you give me your cell phone for a minute? I want to call my answering machine at home to test out our new message," my mother said, changing the subject. An electrical outage had erased my father's outgoing message on the answering machine and my mother had recorded a new one that morning.

"Here, listen to this," she said, handing me back my phone, and

I suddenly heard the clarity of her voice in the short message, even over the sound of the waves.

You have reached Yael and Levi, please leave your message at the sound of the tone, she said, and at that moment, I wanted to connect with her too, to leave her my message.

"Does it sound okay to you?" she asked.

"Perfect."

"I love the water and the sand," my mother said, almost singing, her green eyes turning jade. The beach was my mother's favorite place, the only place her hard edges crumbled with the coastline as it connected with water. Here, she was soft as the sand, and I was happy she was here with me, her voice an antidote to Rhea's notes and letters. I wanted to ask her about them, but I knew it would spoil our day. She suddenly looked tired.

"Didn't you get any sleep last night, Mom?"

"Sometimes I don't sleep . . . for hours."

"What do you do when you don't?"

"You're going to think this is odd, but I name the people I went to elementary school with. I can name them all. I remember every single one of them," she said, as though she was a schoolgirl again.

"That's funny," I said. "When I can't sleep, I sometimes imagine walking through all the apartments and houses I've lived in all over the world. I start at the doorway, and in my mind I walk into every room, trying to remember where everything was. Kind of silly, right?"

My mother smiled. "Not silly at all. And I guess we're not so different after all, are we?" she said with a smile.

Someone walked past us with a long, gauzy beach cover-up, and I thought about the filmy chiffon red dress my mother would wear for concerts.

"What happened to all those dresses you wore on stage? Do you still have them?" I suddenly asked her, the sun warming our blanket on the sand.

"No," she said. "I gave them all away." She paused. "You should come to the opera with me sometime. I'd be happy to buy you an extra ticket."

"I don't know. Our weekends are pretty busy," I mumbled. I didn't want to tell her that I'd read many of the plots but didn't like most of their storylines—the tales of the seductress Carmen, the jealousy that crushed the shepherd in *Acis and Galatea*. Then there was the geisha Butterfly. How could she love the lieutenant who eventually abandoned her? And the cruel Turandot, who decreed death because of an ancient ancestor who was betrayed by a man. Even the storyline of the comedic *Marriage of Figaro* annoyed me. "*Non più andrai, far-fallone amoroso*, no more will you, amorous butterfly, flit around day and night, upsetting all the pretty girls," Figaro sang to his friend Cherubino, who was forced to depart for the army. They were all the same—stories of love and betrayal.

I did love the music, though, when I heard it by chance on the car radio. Somehow it curled up inside of me, finding its way into every part of my body, especially the duets, the separate melodies that fit together like lovers entwined.

"Pretty busy, you say?" My mother repeated my lame attempt at an excuse. "Hmmm," she sighed, and the wind started to pick up. "We should go back," she said.

"Why did you stop singing, Mom?" I asked her, as we got up to leave.

"Did you know that I once sang for the famous conductor, Leonard Bernstein? I sang the aria from the French opera, *Lakmé*, by Delibes. After listening to me, Bernstein said, "Your voice is beautiful, you sing wonderful, but your French is lousy." She laughed, then sighed, and brushed the sand off her pants.

"But all these years after, you could have joined a choir or given voice lessons?"

"Choir? Ach. Voice lessons? That's for amateurs. Singing was all done for me a long time ago," she said, helping me fold up the blanket. "All that is finished."

Eighteen

I drove my mother home, and for the rest of the week, the weather turned gray and blustery, a cloudiness that crept into the corners of the house and even into the car. I was scratching for new ideas, and a few days later, I decided to go back to the antique store where I'd bought the postcard. Maybe there was something I'd missed. Rick, the owner, wasn't there this time, but I knew exactly where to go, and I returned to the same stall, Number 144 in the back of the store, to see if there were any other postcards or letters that might be connected to Maynard or Caldwell. I spent an hour looking through each item on the shelves, sifting through boxes, finding some World War II–era photos of sailors, a ration book belonging to a family in Massachusetts, Valentine cards, and old books, but nothing remotely relating to Maynard. Before I left, I asked the saleswoman for the phone number of the person who owned the stall. She gave me the telephone number for someone named Larry, and I called him and then went to meet him at another small shop he consigned with in West Hollywood.

"Can you show it to me?" Larry said, and he looked closely at the postcard I'd brought along, turning it over, but he couldn't recall. "Doesn't ring any bells. You've got to understand . . . I've collected so many of those postcards over the years."

"Are you sure? Maybe you remember where you might have gotten it? An estate sale in Los Angeles with a Brooklyn connection maybe?"

"Sorry, I wish I could help you. I buy stuff from everywhere, old storage lockers, probate sales. Sometimes I even find boxes in dumpsters or on the street. I wouldn't want to tell you something that would steer you the wrong way."

"Okay. Thanks anyway," I said.

"Hey, this postcard important to you? Some kind of family thing?"

"Well, yes . . . no . . . I don't know."

He looked at me. "That's all right. I get it. Some things stay with you. I'll let you know if I come across anything."

When I returned home, one of the letters I'd sent off to a random North London Maynard came back with a red, waxy slash through the address.

Return to sender, not at this address anymore.

I tore it up.

I was still waiting for the letter from the British Army. I needed distraction and looked at the images of Kentigern House on the internet. It was the building that housed the Army Personnel Centre in Glasgow, Scotland, and I'd imagined it as a hundred-year-old structure, but the Google image depicted a modern building at 65 Brown Street, built in 1986, a large, tiered, sandstone edifice receding inward in a stepped facade, not far from the River Clyde. Then I looked at pictures of examples of army forms on the web. There were Royal Navy certificates of service and War Office forms, discharge records, and certificates. The stained and yellowed forms were filled in with handwriting.

This man bears a good character and is steady and well conducted.

He is sober, steady, reliable and hardworking, intelligent.

What had someone written in Maynard's army file?

I closed my eyes and conjured up some young army clerk digging into the aging filing cabinets for me. A.T. Maynard, the heading on the file would say, alongside his army service number.

A week later, that letter did arrive. I recognized the same brown bag–colored envelope, but smaller this time. *"On Her Majesty's Service"* was printed on the outside. I opened it up and on identical stationary to their previous letter to me, a one-line letter.

> *Regarding Private A.T. Maynard. Your recent e-mails regarding the above named are acknowledged and are receiving attention.*

"Receiving attention?" The sentence was infuriatingly polite, but like the British Army logo on the top left-hand side—two crossed swords beneath a lion balancing on the crown—I too felt poised to pounce. Why couldn't they just tell me outright?

I had a sinking feeling and wished Talia was home. I wanted to show her the letter, and ask her what she thought, but I knew what she would say—that they hadn't actually said no.

~

Ten days later I went out to get the mail. It was almost dark, and I turned on the porch light before gathering up the mail from the box. There were the usual circulars, "Shop Wise" junk mail and Ralphs Supermarket coupons. I almost missed the brown envelope mistakenly tucked in between the Walmart weekend specials. Inside, was what I had been waiting for.

> *Mr. Maynard's forenames are recorded as Arthur Thomas on his service file. I hope that this is useful. Bernadette Hand.*

"Arthur Thomas. Arthur Thomas," I repeated.

The combination of names seemed so natural, so complete, as

if I'd heard them hundreds of times before. He was no longer A.T., a black hole of initials that had kept him hidden away. Arthur. I thought of Arturo in *I Puritani*, an opera set during the English civil war of the 1640s. Arturo was condemned to death by his Parliament, and his love, Elvira, descended into madness, thinking he was in love with another woman. Despite the risk to his life, though, Arturo stole into Elvira's garden to assure Elvira he loved only her. I couldn't have hoped for a better name for my A.T. Arturo was a man joyful to be reunited with his beloved, a man who had never betrayed his woman.

"Look at this," I said, running over to Talia who had just come home. I showed her the letter. "I want to dance. Dance with me?"

"This is so great, Mom, but now?" She laughed. "I've got to get ready for Karen's party."

"C'mon. Please," I said, tugging at her arm. "Show me some hip-hop?"

"Well, all right," she said, getting up, "But not hip-hop. I'll teach you to swing dance." She took my hand and showed me a few steps. "This is East Coast swing. I'll lead, and you follow," she directed me, and I focused on her instructions.

Then she put a CD in her boom box.

"I love this," I said, hearing the 1940s 4/4 time swing tempo.

"Triple step, triple step, and then rock step," she drilled, and I tried to follow her lead. "Keep the steps small, and don't hold on to me too tight," she coached. "Just trust me to move you."

We swung back and forth, the motion propelled by the momentum of our bodies coming together and apart, and we danced around the living room, laughing as we bumped into the couch and the end tables. Then we moved the furniture out of the way and practiced spins and swing outs, jitterbugging and twisting away, breathless with the music.

I closed my eyes, and we danced for a while, the two of us, mirror images of each other, but the feeling remained, mysterious, that there was someone else in the room, another person dancing with us.

Nineteen

I dug under the pile of papers on my desk and found the British electoral CD-ROM I'd tried out with my mother awhile back. This time though, I had more than just initials—I had a first and middle name, and I entered the information. The CD listed twenty-two Arthur Maynards throughout England, Scotland, and Wales. They were from all over—from Bristol to Cornwall, Manchester to Kent. They lived on roads and streets, drives and lanes, and I used the UK StreetMap website to find each of the addresses, tracing the nearby roads with the tip of my finger. I wrote letters to each Arthur Maynard and addressed twenty-two envelopes.

The next day, I took the letters with me to work. Walking toward the post office during my lunch break, I stopped to sit on one of the few remaining benches in the courthouse plaza. Much of the plaza had been fenced off for renovation, and there was a mess of stucco pallets and wooden two-by-fours.

I sat in the shadow of the ivory-colored Van Nuys City Hall and its eight-story central tower, which culminated in a concrete dome. Built in the thirties, it was designed to be a replica of its sister city hall in downtown Los Angeles. But now the boarded-up windows were surrounded with dusty fencing.

It reminded me of the ruined park scene near the castle in Donizetti's opera *Lucia de Lammermoor*, the tale of the feud between the Scottish families of Ravenswood and Lammermoor. In the opera, Enrico's fortunes were waning, and he tried to force his sister, Lucia, to marry Lord Arthur Ashton. Lucia, in love with Edgardo, was shown a forged letter and eventually yielded to her brother's wishes. But in the end, Lucia went mad and killed Arthur, then died herself, her lover stabbing himself to join her in death. I looked at the stack of letters in my hand.

Would the letters find their way to Arthur Maynard or his family, and even if they did, what story would I find?

With only a few minutes left of my lunch break, I walked toward the chorus line of bail bondsmen and law offices of Van Nuys Boulevard, past a sheriff inspecting tinted windows and loud mufflers, then toward the local TV vans covering some celebrity trial. I dropped the twenty-two letters inside the mail slot of the post office and headed back to work.

"Hey there," a colleague named Michael called out from behind me, then caught up to me. "Going to the judges meeting at two o'clock?"

I stopped and turned around. "Yes, on my way now."

"Hey, I heard about some little postcard project you were doing. Some Nancy Drew sleuthing on the side?"

"Where did you hear that?"

"Mark told me."

"Mark told you?" Great. Who else had Mark told? And was I now the butt of the judges' lounge joke?

"You wouldn't want to piss off the presiding judge, would you?" he said, laughing.

"Well—" I began, wondering whether I should be concerned.

But suddenly a breeze kicked up between the two courthouses. Not strong enough to create the wind tunnel that often roared between the two buildings, but a benign breeze that blew away the leaves, and strong enough that I could almost feel it lifting me, propping me up.

It seemed to drive away any worries I'd had about stickler presiding judges, reassignments, and teasing colleagues.

"Oh, that? Who knows? Maybe I would," I said, and continued walking. "Come on, we'll be late."

The black gates at the entrance of my high school were made of intricate ironwork, and the driveway led to a covered portico underneath the bulging eyes of stone gargoyles. The old mansion housed a small Jewish school on the Main Line in Philadelphia. But it had been built in the early part of the last century, and it too had a name, Drake Linden Hall. Inside, there was a central staircase of carved wood, and in many of the classrooms, the old fireplaces and moldings had been saved. Everywhere there were little niches and hiding places, and even a crooked stairway that led to the attic. It was a perfect backdrop for a black-and-white film noir, and before it became a school, it had also been the setting for a gritty 1950s Jane Mansfield movie called The Burglar.

I loved the old building and mossy grounds. Last period, I'd go to the school library and sit on the floor between the tall stacks. Surrounded by books, I'd make up stories of ghosts and secrets. Had the library once been the dining room where butlers went back and forth with silver trays? Was there a lover's tryst between the chauffeur and the maid in the basement, which now only housed the cafeteria, the school lockers, and the science labs?

And who had lived in the last bedroom upstairs with a lock on the door and a broken windowpane that let in a breeze?

Twenty

Dearest Daddy. *Don't be disturbed but understand we don't want to share these pictures or their meaning with <u>no one</u>. This is just for you and me. I do think you owe me that much, Daddy. The picture we wish to send Grandmother Rachel we will send to her. I talk about you in my sleep and kiss you.*

It had taken me a full hour to psych myself up to open it again; still my stomach churned when I read it, this, the fourth note in the file. What pictures? What meaning? I could no longer keep the file to myself. I photocopied the entire thing and mailed off the copies to my brother.

I had the rest of the day to myself and drove out to the Family History Library in West Los Angeles. It belonged to the Church of Latter-Day Saints, and I knew only members of the church could enter the temple, but the library was open to the public. My ideas for new research avenues dwindling, any help, even from those saints who barred me from their temple, would be welcome.

The church was on a hill and crowned Santa Monica Boulevard. It was a Taj Mahal–like mausoleum of manicured gardens, where the angel Moroni blew a golden horn and the gods of genealogy now resided. An elevator took me down to the floor below where there was a cave of microfilm machines, old-fashioned spoolers, and census records spanning hundreds of years in metal, floor-to-ceiling cabinets, all meticulously indexed and cross-referenced.

A volunteer named Janet taught me how to use the microfilm reader, how to roll up the spools and see the image on the special carrel. I found the 1901 British Census, the latest released, probably twenty years before the private was born, I figured. But even if Maynard's father appeared on the census, how would I even be able to identify him? Starting with Arthur as a forename, a cursory search revealed more than fifty Arthur Maynards on the 1901 Census, and these were in every part of the UK. I tried another approach. There was no guarantee Maynard had actually lived in Tottenham, but it was a starting point. There were sixteen Maynards listed for the parish, which was in the county of Middlesex. I asked for a photocopy of the list.

About a week later, I drove to another library, this time the Central Public Library. Downtown Los Angeles was almost deserted on a Sunday, a ghost town. The interior of the library was dark, the building like a sphinx with snake motifs and a tiled rooftop pyramid. A procession of down escalators through an eight-story glass atrium led me to the history department. I had no idea what exactly I was looking for but ordered some *LIFE* magazines from March to April 1942. More than the articles themselves, the wartime advertisements gave the flavor of the times. *We're backing them up*, declared a Bell Telephone ad. *The Place of Home in the Morale of the Nation*, Hoover vacuums reminded. *For America Behind the Guns*, proclaimed the Sunsweet Prune Juice advertisement. The April 20, 1942, cover depicted a model in slacks—*a craze that has swept the nation. Men lose their pants to slacks-crazy women.* There were ads for cigarettes too, brands I'd never heard of—Spud Imperials and Julep Mint for *when war worries and defense activities keep nerves tense.*

Two hours later, I left thinking I'd fallen into more time-wasting rabbit holes.

The next day, an email arrived from a Mark Maynard.

I am sorry to say that I cannot help you trace Arthur Thomas Maynard, he wrote. *I have no knowledge of any relation with those Christian names, or who served in the RASC during the Second World War. I hope you achieve success with other Maynards.*

I received another email, three days later from another Maynard.

I'm writing on behalf of my father, Arthur Colston Maynard. Unfortunately, I don't think we can help you. My dad didn't serve during the war, and the only other Arthur Maynard we know of was a docker in Cardiff throughout the war years. Sorry we can't help you any further—and thanks for making the effort to get in touch (even if it was with the wrong family!)

More email trickled in, one from a Dr. Maynard.

Thank you for your letter. Interestingly, both my father and I have the middle name Arthur inherited from my grandfather whose own father had it as a middle name. Unfortunately, neither my father or I have heard of this person.

Finally, three more emails from a Thomas Maynard in Surrey, Tom Maynard from the Isle of Man, and Neil Maynard in Sunderland. I printed them all out and put them away in a burgeoning folder that I marked with a big NOT in black marker.

～

It was Talia who brought the small envelope into the house one afternoon. It was in an unfamiliar handwriting, addressed to me, and as I opened it, I was certain it was another crossed wire, a letter of regret from another wrong Maynard. I read the letter out loud to Talia.

Dear Madam,
Thank you for your letter of 26th Jan 04.

Yes! I did know a British Army Private ARTHUR THOMAS MAYNARD, RASC 1942. He was my father. Of course I have no way of knowing if the person you mention and my father are one and the same. Although I am sure you will agree it is a strange coincidence.

However, I leave it entirely to your discretion how you handle the matter, but must say I am very intrigued. I am his next of kin, being his eldest son, and I thank you for writing to me.

Sincerely,
A.E. Maynard (Mr.) Arthur Edward Maynard

"Call him. Call him right now," Talia said, grabbing the phone, and handing it to me.

I looked at the letter carefully. It was written on stationery, folded twice, the paper a shade of pastel green, almost celadon. The handwriting was slanted to the left, each *y* joyful. There was even an exclamation mark, like the one on the postcard, maybe a sign, a peculiarity passed on from father to son? But there it was—*He was my father.* If the solider of the postcard had been this person's father, he had passed away. I didn't want to think about it.

"But there's no phone number. Not even an email address," I said, reading the letter again. There was only a return postal address in a town called Thetford, in Norfolk. "It's going to take forever to get an answer back," I said, putting the phone down.

"That's not so bad. Maybe it'll give you time to take it all in," Talia said.

Talia was right. I was becoming addicted to an instantaneous world, impatient even as the hourglass icon appeared on my screen to tell me it was loading up a page, annoyed when the "send" button took more than four seconds to obey my command. Email was fast food, filling, but it had robbed me of reflection.

I sat at the kitchen table and wrote him a long letter. I told him about myself and my family, and how I'd found the postcard by chance in a thrift store. I asked him if he would look through his father's belongings to see whether he could confirm the British Army serial number. After I was done, I went to the post office to send the letter by express mail. I fired off an instant message to Bert in Australia.

"Where the hell is Thetford?" I emailed Bert, who had become my go-to person on all things and places British.

After the war, I spent some time at a transit camp, on an ex-American bomber aerodrome named Knettishall, and the local town was, believe it or not, Thetford, Bert wrote back.

Minutes later, I went on the internet and searched out the town of Thetford. It was a principal stopping place on the main coach road from London to Norwich, I learned, a city of wooden bridges and black-and-white, timber-framed buildings. The county of Norfolk was known for its ghosts and ghouls, from the headless coachman of Blickling Hall, to a phantom monk who appeared at Norwich's Maddermarket Theater. The town was also the birthplace of American patriot Thomas Paine and the stomping grounds of the Maharajah Duleep Singh who ruled the Punjab in 1843 before coming to live as a country gentleman at nearby Elveden estate. Another Maharajah? There was sure to be a connection to the one involved in the Tobacco Fund, right?

I learned everything I could about the county and town, and

began planning the train ride to Thetford, checking train schedules and reading up on the local gossip and church schedules in the village newsletter on the web.

Over the next few weeks, the wait for the confirmation was excruciating. Why didn't he have an email address? Why hadn't he included his phone number? I carped about snail mail to anyone who would listen until my own email box was suddenly hacked. A tech from my server explained that my spam filters had been tricked, "spoofed," he'd said. "To" and "from" had been manipulated to allow bulk mail to pass, he wrote. There were pop-ups and a slew of viruses, and I had to delete hundreds of emails. But worse than that, a week later, some cyber glitch had disconnected my internet service, and I spent two hours under my desk with the outsourced Dell Help Desk wonk, disconnecting and reconnecting cables, and reporting what lights were on or off on my SpeedStream modem.

Finally after a long month, I received the letter from Thetford I'd been waiting for, and I tore it open on the doorstep.

I have no way of confirming my father's British Army serial number. I would probably recognize his handwriting if that would help but that, I'm afraid, that is all I can offer you in your search.

What now?

A friend urged me to tell the man to make a formal request to the British Army for his father's record and serial number. "You need a solid confirmation," he strongly counseled. "You have to be careful. Anyone can claim the postcard belonged to them. Without a serial number, you can't be sure."

But I didn't want to be cautious, or think about legalities for once. I wanted to believe that the man from Thetford was Arthur Maynard's son. Besides, I knew from my own experience that it would take months for him to get any kind of confirmation from the British Army, and I was too impatient to wait that long.

I put down the phone and made a copy of the postcard to send to the Thetford Maynard. But would he recognize the handwriting? Just then, Talia came home from school. I watched her as she tossed her backpack on the kitchen table. It landed sharply, like a rap on a door, and I no longer had any doubt. I could almost hear the fates and even those Latter Day Saints finally aligning as she kicked off her shoes and threw open the refrigerator, her hands stretched out in the air.

It was the end of the summer, 1969. An American astronaut had landed on the moon, Woodstock was in full swing back in the States, and I was on a two-day layover on the way back from Israel with my parents. I'd just turned seventeen on my first trip abroad, and London was everything suburban Philadelphia wasn't. We toured Westminster Abbey and Big Ben, but there was also Carnaby Street and Twiggy, all a million miles away from split-level houses, plastic-covered sofas, and fruit-filled Jell-O molds. At breakfast, I giggled when a waitress called me "luv," and I bought glossy postcards to send to my friends back home. And then there were the gardens of Windsor Castle, the soft rain, streets full of umbrellas, and the Victoria Memorial, her golden arms outstretched in a statue called Winged Victory.

Twenty-one

$\mathbb{I}$ was wrong about the fates aligning.

Another four weeks went by and the Thetford Maynard replied.

> *My wife and I have enjoyed reading your letters, but the post-card you sent sadly is not my father's hand. I am sorry to disappoint you, and sorry we are not connected to your Pte. A.T. Maynard.*

The next day, a tropical storm hung sluggish over Baja in the south, but the storm seemed to reach northward, even to Los Angeles, and the clouds fell limp, like swaths of wet cloth falling from the sky. It was strange weather for Los Angeles, usually desert-dry.

At least you know for sure that he's not your Maynard, Bert wrote to me, trying to console me, offering to call the British Army from Australia himself on my behalf and see if they would release more information. *And if he's not the right one, your Maynard may still be alive.* He then attached a photograph of himself and his late wife, Elsa, taken on their wedding day in 1952.

Kay too wrote to me from Brooklyn. *Don't give up*, Kay wrote. *Le coeur a des raisons que la raison ne connait pas.* The heart has reasons that reason does not know.

But I was sick of it all. My search was going nowhere. I already had two journals full of useless notes and clippings. I couldn't stand to write or print out any more letters with the same, stale inquiry. Maybe I'd never been meant to find Arthur Maynard. Maybe I'd only been meant to find my cyber friends, Bert and Kay.

It was hot in the house, and Talia and I decided to drive north to Ventura to get away from the muggy heat.

I drove for about an hour, but the clouds remained, a sky of cracked eggshells now, unusually humid and steamy. On the way, across greenish strawberry fields, workers carried long tubing over their shoulders, stepping silently into the furrows to plant strawberries.

"I can't do it anymore. I can't write to all the freaking Maynards in the UK. There are more than two thousand," I blurted out to Talia as we drove up the coast, but she was listening to music on her iPod and didn't hear me.

We were close to the Ventura Harbor now, a string of boatyards and cranes, a chandlery selling cordage and canvas, another store offering charts and navigation supplies. I parked the car and we walked around the manmade harbor.

"I don't know what else I can do," I said as we passed the launch ramp.

"I'll type up some envelopes for you when we get home, if you want," Talia offered.

"You want to help?" I asked Talia.

"You don't always have to do everything yourself, Mom," Talia said. "I can help. Just ask."

The red-tiled shops catered mostly to weekend tourists. A carousel wheezed from somewhere, challenging the sounds of a loud video arcade. Talia bought a cowrie shell bracelet in a store filled with blown glass knickknacks and coral lining the shelves, fishnet falling in swells from the ceiling.

"What about the Thomas Maynards?" she said, turning to me. "Have you written to them yet?" Talia asked. "Maybe Arthur would have given a son his middle name."

I hadn't thought of that, and her idea gave me some hope. Later, we ate fish and chips at an outdoor restaurant, sitting on a playground-yellow table attached to an orbit of seats. Out near the water, the line of boats seemed to melt together in the ebbing light, and as the air cooled off more, the harbor filled up with people. We finished eating and watched the sun set in the west, the marina glowing in the twilight like fired pottery. Talia was about to stand up when I pulled a piece of paper out of my handbag.

"I want to show you something," I said. I didn't know why, but suddenly it felt like the right time to let her see it, here near the water's edge.

"See what?"

I handed her a copy I'd made of the first page of the Rhea file. She glanced at it and then looked at me.

"You found this?"

"More like took it." I told her about the day I filched the file off the floor of my parents' house. She was quiet as she read the notes one by one.

"This is so sad, Mom. So sad. But I get it now."

"Get what?"

"I totally get the whole postcard thing."

"What do you mean the whole postcard thing?"

"It's kind of obvious."

"No, I really don't understand."

"Mom, these notes about secrets, and the way Rhea underlined those words, and then a few days later you find some random postcard in some random place with 'do not disclose' underlined. I get why you wanted to find this guy. I didn't get it all this time, but now I understand." On her wrist, the delicate cowrie shells were smooth and shiny, and perfectly connected one to another. She was right.

"Understand?" I echoed. "I'm not even sure I do. You're right about the underlining. That's what first drew me to it, but somehow, it's more than that. I just have a feeling that the postcard isn't the end of the story, that there's more to it than just a thank you. That it was the beginning of another story. Don't ask me why."

"Don't lose hope about finding him, Mom. Let's take a walk near the boats before we go home," she proposed, and we crossed a long, dark stretch of grass toward the marina. As we were walking, I suddenly realized my cell phone had slipped out of my hand.

"I dropped it," I said, and we retraced our steps, but I couldn't find it. I started to get edgy. "We're never going to find it," I complained.

"Just wait," Talia said.

"Wait for what? Even if you call it, we won't hear it ringing. It's too noisy here." There was the constant sound of seagulls in the distance, interrupted only by a man with a karaoke-like microphone announcing fish orders ready for pick up.

"Just wait until it gets a little darker," she said, and we sat down together on the grass waiting for the sky to dim.

I looked out toward the Channel Islands, fourteen miles away. Only a hint of their outlines was visible; Anacapa, what the Chumash called the Island of Deception, would be soon swallowed up by the dusk. I hadn't noticed Talia had taken out her cell and was making a call.

"There it is, Mom," she said, pointing to a spot, and I could see it too, my lost cell phone, just a little glint, lighting up with Talia's call.

A week after my eighteenth birthday, my parents drove me to New York, and I boarded a night flight to Tel Aviv. On the plane, I saw New York City lit up below me. Soon, the lights disappeared, and with them the things I'd left behind: my family, the restraints of religion, and the vague feeling that something in those eighteen years had been amiss.

I was part of a group of forty freshmen from all over the US, about to start studies at Hebrew University in Jerusalem, and I sat next to a blonde girl I didn't know for the ten-hour flight to Tel Aviv. Somewhere over Canada, she opened up a bottle of perfume and dabbed herself behind her ear; then she took out a round, pastel-colored thing that looked like my grandmother's face powder compact, but when she opened it up, there was no powder, only tiny pills arranged in a circle.

After we landed, we took a bus to an agricultural school in the north, and for two weeks, we hiked and visited ancient Roman ruins as a prelude to the school year. We came back with blistered feet and sunburns and fell into our beds exhausted.

But at night, in the girls' dormitory of cots, and in the whispers of their stories, I made sure not to fall asleep so I could listen closely to learn the magic of perfumes and pills.

Twenty-two

When we came back to the house, Talia wanted to immediately look up all the Thomas Maynards on the CD-ROM.

"There are exactly thirty-seven," she announced, and she printed out all the letters and envelopes for me. "All you have to do this time is mail them."

Ten days later, several emails came back.

Unfortunately, I am not able to be of help to you.

Sorry, but as far as I can see, this particular Thomas Maynard is not a relation.

I'm unable to shed light on the subject.

I have no knowledge of Pte. Arthur Maynard.

There was nothing more for me to do but wait again, and another week went by.

On my way back from visiting a friend in the city one Saturday, the 405 freeway took me past the Los Angeles National Cemetery in Westwood. Bordering the freeway on one side and UCLA on the other, the cemetery had veterans from wars dating as far back as the Civil War interred along the neat rows. A bright afternoon spread across the thousands of gravestones, markers almost blinding white as I started to make my way up the foothills of the Santa Monica Mountains. I must have passed the 114-acre cemetery dotted with Spanish-style buildings hundreds of times, never stopping, but today it somehow called out to me, and I exited the freeway, backtracking to the entrance. There, I stopped to buy flowers from a guy hawking bouquets wrapped in plastic and parked under a tree.

Outside my car, a hot spring sun beat down across the blue sky, the freeway a whining river of cars nearby.

What was I doing here?

There were thousands of white gravestones, and I read them one by one as I passed. I wanted to put the flowers on someone's grave, but whose? There were so many, and I walked from plot to plot. Each marker told another story, of a father or son, lost, reduced now only to stone. One stood misaligned, abutting against the trunk of a tree, once a sapling, but now full grown.

Finally, I came across Williams, O.H., who died in 1931. His gravestone was the least descriptive, only his last name and first and second initials, and the date he was killed. There was no rank or military branch, no mention of when he was born, and like my Maynard, there was nothing to tell me whether he'd been a father, husband, or brother.

I bent down and put my flowers for Williams, O.H.

∽

When I returned home, I had an email from Maria in New York. *I found this tiny mention of a W. Caldwell in the* Brooklyn Daily Eagle *in September of 1950. It probably isn't very helpful to you, but I thought I'd pass it along anyway,* she wrote.

> *At 7:00 p.m. yesterday, a fire broke out in one of the apartments at 275 Clinton. At this time, cause unknown. The*

owner, a W. Caldwell, stated that the fire destroyed some rugs, furniture, and paintings in his living room. When asked if the paintings were valuable, the shaken Caldwell replied, "Not really, but they were sentimental, some watercolors, just a gift from a friend."

Maria was right. Even though it mentioned W. Caldwell at the same address, the article didn't seem to point to any important information.

But a few weeks later, in April, almost to the day and month the postcard had been written more than sixty years ago, there was an email in my inbox from someone I didn't recognize.

How you managed to track me down is a mystery, but I am grateful for your letter of the 10ᵗʰ· My sister and I are the two remaining of a large family, and our eldest brother was Arthur Thomas Maynard, and he served as a private around 1942 in the RASC. He died in 1963 at the age of fifty-four, never having married.

Again, this Arthur was gone.
I read on.

We cannot imagine what the item is that you have discovered, but we do know that he had a great love of the arts, particularly writing and painting. I am sending you this e-mail from a friend's computer, and if you reply here I'm sure he would get it to me. I have moved from the Bedford address. Tom Maynard.

Died in 1963? If this was the postcard's A.T. Maynard, I was forty years late. But when I printed the email out and reread it, it seemed that fate had found a way to intervene. Despite a wrong address for him, my letter had somehow been forwarded and reached Tom. And there was another consolation. There was a sweetness to the email, a hopefulness in Tom's words, of love and a large family, of art, writing, and discovery.

Maybe it wasn't too late.

I scanned the postcard, and attached it to my email.

It wasn't more than a day later, another email from Tom—

The writing is unmistakable, and I attach a copy of a page of a letter from him to me in, I think 1961. I also attach a piece of artwork, a watercolor, of his from around the same time.

A watercolor? Like the article from the Brooklyn newspaper Maria had described to me? Could there really have been more than a postcard connection between Maynard and Caldwell? I placed the postcard next to the letter Tom had attached for me and knew I didn't need to confirm the serial number or hire a handwriting expert. Even to my lay eyes, the handwriting, its looping calligraphy so distinct, was a match. I reread the excerpt from Arthur's letter. It appeared to be a page from a longer letter written in 1961.

Everything I love and value and hold dear seems to be held up to ridicule, or destroyed. Everything I hate and abhor seems to flourish, at home, at work, and all around me.

But the sample watercolor was more cheerful, a bouquet of flowers and a poem from Wordsworth in calligraphy. *We'll talk of sunshine and of song and summer days when we were young.*

There was a flurry of emails back and forth to Tom, and to Michael and Valerie, Tom's neighbors who had facilitated my correspondence with Tom. Valerie wrote that Tom lived in Stibbard, a tiny hamlet near the town of Fakenham. Tom suffered from emphysema, she also wrote, which sometimes left him breathless. It was good I was coming soon, she added.

He has a real treasure trove of old family relics, and a huge folder of letters from his brother, and lots of his brother's watercolors. I hope you will find what you are looking for.

There wasn't much on the internet about the village of Stibbard, just someone's personal web page with a few photos of the All Saints Primary School and church, a village hall, and the village sign, a ploughman with his horse plough, constructed from old iron objects found on a farm.

In late April, I set up a time to call Tom. An hour before, David called me from work.

"Good luck," he said.

"I'm kind of nervous."

"Don't be. You're just nervous about the abundance in your life," he said. "You're not used to that."

"You're right. I'm not."

I called Tom at exactly twelve thirty Pacific Time. We spoke for more than an hour. It was eight hours later in England, and I immediately loved the soft inflection in his voice, the breaths he took, up and down, like organ pipes.

"I was so surprised to get your letter," he said, but there was no astonishment in his voice, as though he'd been expecting me. He then told me a little about the Maynard clan.

They were a close-knit family with working-class roots, and had lived in the North London suburb of Tottenham. Arthur was born in 1909. Their mother was an illegitimate child, her father unknown. There were originally seven brothers and sisters, two died early on, and four brothers, one sister remained.

"Arthur was always reading the classics, even though he only had an elementary education. He had a girlfriend for a while, but never married, working at odd jobs, a postman and loader and various other office jobs. He went from job to job, and lived in rented rooms with another brother, or sleeping on friends' floors."

"I can't wait to see you," I said, toward the end of our conversation.

"Yes, I'm very much looking forward to it. You know, Leora, I think we were meant to discover each other," he said, and I felt it too, the strangest of connections, like an inconspicuous link on a website, a random click, converging and taking me to a place I didn't know I needed to go.

It was another three-day layover in London, this time on my way back to the States for a visit after my first year of law school in Jerusalem, a last-minute student ticket Sharon, a schoolmate, and I had cobbled together. It turned out to be a good way to put distance between me and the tumult of an on-and-off first love that had come in the form of a young Jewish convert from Holland. Raised as a minister's son, he'd only later discovered his secret Jewish bloodline, hidden during Nazi occupation of the Netherlands, his story of wartime secrets and melancholy drawing me into a hazily familiar flame.

It was summer, warm for London, and Sharon and I found our way to Trafalgar Square and Piccadilly Circus. Then, to get away from the heat, we decided to see a matinee at a smoke-filled cinema nearby. The next day, on a boat ride on the Thames, we met a backpacker, and the three of us spent the day together, talking and laughing, taking photos of one another as though we were old friends. At dinner, he asked if he could crash on the floor of our hotel room on his sleeping bag for one night, and we said okay.

But before dawn, I woke up with the smack of our hotel door closing. I looked around the room. He was gone, his backpack and sleeping bag too, not even a note, as though he'd never been there. I went to the window and looked out, but there was no trace of him, only the sound of the Thames nearby to remind us of him.

"Pretty weird, right?" I said to Sharon.

"I don't know," she said, yawning. "Sometimes people just need to go."

Twenty-three

"I read it all," Ron said. It was early morning on a Sunday and I was putting fresh sheets on my bed when my brother called. "I read everything in the file all at once. Twice."

I sat down on the unmade bed. "That's better than me. I couldn't get myself to read more than one note at a time. I haven't even gotten to the letters or that postcard from Florida." I'd only glanced at the glossy blue of the cloudless Miami sky.

"This one letter really got to me," he said. "I have to read it to you. You have to hear this," Ron said.

"Now?"

"Just listen," he insisted.

I put the phone on speaker and put it on the bed while Ron read it out loud.

My dearest Daddy, how do you like my badge? It was given to me by the lifeguard for holding my breath under the water. He made me an underwater member. I eat only kosher and say my prayers every night. Mommy and I say the blessings over the candles and drink wine on Friday nights. Why does Mommy always cry?

I started to feel light-headed.

"We can never show these to Mom," Ron said.

"You think she doesn't know about the file?" I asked.

"I don't know. She's always been a pretty good detective, but I hope she never saw it, and will never see it."

"I hope so too," I echoed, and then I hung up. Suddenly I realized my father's secret had now become mine too. Who to tell? Who to share it with? Or do I keep it hidden away, making me his aider and abettor?

I put the phone back in its cradle and looked at my unmade bed. The images in the note swirled in my head—a little girl learning how to swim and learning how to hold her breath under the water, a little girl saying her prayers, and a mother who writes notes and letters in the voice of her child. Was it desperation on Rhea's part or manipulation? Or both?

The mattress remained bare, the sheets still folded, and I curled up into a ball, the layers of tufts and steel coils both hard and soft sinking beneath me as though I was underwater holding my breath too.

~

Later, after a long walk, I hoped to take Talia out to lunch, but she wasn't home yet from practice. I called her on her cell phone and left a message.

While I waited for her to return my call, I went on the internet and checked out every London webcam I could find. There were livestreams from Oxford Circus and Covent Gardens, views of Trafalgar Square updated every five seconds. Buses stood still and then reappeared on the other side of the square, real time in a bizarre, languid delay. I counted thirty-one working traffic cameras in central London, and I visited each one. It was night there, and the streets were almost empty, and each location exuded its own tint of color, some blue-black, others canary yellow. Buses were lit up from the inside, and streetlamps looked like tiny, bright gems. In one fish-eye lens, a lone person crossed the street, his arm raised to hail a cab, and a taxi stopped, but it was as though some video frames had gone missing. In an instant, the person was gone, consumed into the cab.

An email popped up in a box on my screen from Valerie in Norfolk. *Tom is in the hospital*, she wrote, and my heart stopped.

But don't be alarmed. He is doing fine and hopes to be home at the weekend. But his breathing was so bad that his nephew had to call the paramedics, and they took him straight to hospital.

I stared at the screen for a long time. Tom was sick?
His breathing was so bad.

I logged off and dug out the Rhea file again. This time I went through the entire file, taking in all its contents. There were just a few more notes and a short news article about Rhea cut out from a Philadelphia newspaper, and other letters she'd written my father. There was also a photocopy of a journal my father had kept, with dates and amounts, but the notations were all written in Romanian, and I couldn't make out what the notations said.

Last, there was a postcard.

It had never been mailed, the tiny writing bleeding over to where it said "place stamp here." It was from the Fontainebleau Hotel, the "F" in fancy cursive. "America's largest and finest resort-hotel, cabana and yacht club, on the former Firestone estate," the postcard boasted. "A masterpiece of design, air conditioned comfort and hospitality supreme, curving majestically above the ocean and bay. Open all year." The date at the top was faint, but it looked like March 1959.

Remembering you this Purim, and I can think of nothing better for you than to PRAY. May your eyes see the light, your ears hear the deep truth—your mind lead you to justness—and *with your heart—receive the unselfish love. I too pray here for your forgiveness. My little heart is a true creation of perfect union of love. Everyone that sees her must say a word of love to her. She is everyone's darling and no one to claim her—only me, her **sick** mother. The little one was sick Friday night. I had to leave our dinner and bring her back to bed. She is better now—I think she is lonely for you. She calls for you all the time. She tells me how much she wants to see you—but she may get over it—and I sort of feel sorry for that affection to be lost.*

I closed my eyes. My stomach lurched, and I was feeling sick too.

I'd had enough of postcards and files, researching and digging into secrets. The room seemed to spin around, and I could almost smell it—the suntan lotion mixed with perfume on Rhea's skin. I could imagine him, my father, sitting on a balcony of the Fontainebleau Hotel, staring out across Biscayne Bay.

If Tom was too sick to see me, there was still time to cancel the trip. Maybe Valerie was trying to tell me not to come.

I came back to Israel from summer vacation in Philadelphia just a few days before the war. It was October 1973, and Jerusalem was blacked out, and even the car headlights were wrapped and taped up with black paper. Dorm-less, I found myself in someone's empty apartment, alone for the night, the rooms so dark I couldn't catch a sliver of light anywhere. I finally fell asleep below a window, waking up to a nightmare about my second ex-boyfriend who'd been called up to reserve duty at the front lines. I tried to get word of him but couldn't reach anyone, and even though we'd parted months earlier, the nightmare had extinguished all the rough edges of our time together, edges of secrets and the darkness of other wars, and I decided I had to get to the northern border to find out if he was okay.

I hitchhiked and somehow in the chaos of jeeps and convoys on the road, I found his unit. He was all right, but it was already night, too late for me to go back to Jerusalem, and that night we stayed in a small hotel on the outskirts of Safed that had been requisitioned by the army. All night, Katyusha rockets rained down closer and closer. First came their soft whine across the sky, then the jolt of their explosions. And with each, a silence between us, pushing us farther apart.

"You shouldn't have come," he finally turned to me and said, just a voice in the black of the night.

"You're right," I answered, but only when dawn finally crept in. "I shouldn't have come."

Twenty-four

On the Sunday of Memorial Day weekend, my mother called.

"Let's take a drive somewhere," she proposed.

"I'm not really up to it," I mumbled into the phone, sure that the invite was just a pretense to cross-examine me as to why I'd been dodging her calls for the last few days.

"You come here, and I'll drive," she volunteered, and I knew for certain that something was up. My mother almost never offered to drive. "Come on," she insisted. "It'll give us a chance to talk."

"I really don't want to talk, Mom."

"Ah, so now you don't want to talk."

"I know you're still upset."

I was sure she was still annoyed with me about Dena's short visit to Los Angeles last week and the fact that Dena had stayed with me. I hadn't seen her in years, but she was exactly as I remembered her, still blonde, with a cherubic face that now, working as a doula, ushered babies gently into the world. We'd hugged for a long time at my door.

"You think I should have let her come to see him at *my* house, don't you? You can't understand me, Leora. No one can understand me."

The mantra was becoming a line in the sand between us. "You keep saying that. But really? They had to meet at a Starbucks?"

I thought about the judicial ethics course I'd taken at a Van Nuys airport hotel a few weeks ago, and the checklist that had been handed out on Day-Glo green paper about avoiding arguments or personalizing an encounter, and using clear rules and boundaries.

But there were no clear rules and boundaries when it came to dealing with my mother, except for the unambiguous limits she'd constructed for herself.

"Mom, I think—"

"Listen to me. I think I've been more than reasonable. Your father and Dena can see one another whenever they want, just not in *my* house."

"Look, we've been over this again and again," I argued. "Dena's also the victim in all this too, just like you, just like the rest of us. She didn't ask to be born. And she's not her mother."

I suddenly thought about Rhea's letter, and I felt my stomach boil. "Never mind," I said. "Let's not talk about it anymore." I wanted to tell her again that I could love them both—both my mother and my half sister—that loving one didn't have to mean not loving the other, but I didn't say it. I'd said it so many other times before.

"I'll be waiting for you," she said and then hung up.

Later, in my mother's Ford Escort, the street took on the same muted color of her car's beige interior. She was also wearing a cream-colored suit, a matching handbag and shoes, and she seemed to dissolve into the seat. It was hot in the car, and my face throbbed red from the sun, my palms sticky, but my mother remained unruffled, as if she'd been sitting in a cool breeze. Ahead of us, a man on a tall unicycle crossed Pico Boulevard, oddly misplaced on the busy street. Precarious on his high perch, he balanced like a circus clown. I watched my mother's face as she drove, her purse flat and small on her spotless lap. Unlike me, she never carried a large purse, managing with very little, as if she'd made a purposeful decision to whittle down her needs. It seemed a strange confidence, almost a determination—to survive life solely on her wits.

"Where are we going?" I asked, pulling my hair back into a ponytail.

"Nowhere special. It's nice just to drive around, yes?"

The Escort was the first car that was exclusively her own and not shared with my father, and she loved the personalized license plate Ron had arranged for her—4YAEL.

She drove carefully with two hands perfectly centered on the steering wheel, one on each side, and I thought of the long drives I'd taken with Rhea. How different the geography of Rhea's hands, one barely touching the bottom of the steering wheel, the other leaning easily out the open window.

A few minutes later, we were under the 405 Freeway near an off-ramp. Ahead, a long line of cars was stopped at a red light, and we inched our way forward. Finally, the light turned green.

"You do have some kind of destination in mind for this ride, don't you?" I asked.

"Well . . ." My mother seemed distracted by my question. She hesitated at the green light until someone honked from behind. Then, just as we drove away from the overpass, something fell from the freeway above, and my mother applied the brakes. A pallet of white powder landed barely inches from the car's front bumper.

"See," my mother exclaimed. "See that? If you hadn't asked me a question and I hadn't hesitated, that thing would have come down right on us. I was thinking about you. That's what stopped it from happening . . . it was you who did it," she said. "You did it by asking me a question," she repeated, as though she was reciting a mathematical equation.

"It was just dumb luck. And it probably wouldn't have caused any damage anyway."

"No, it wasn't luck," she insisted.

"But nothing happened."

"It's not always what happens that's crucial. What doesn't happen is just as important," she said. "Did you know I had an audition at the New York Metropolitan Opera. "*The Met*, can you imagine? It was my *one* best chance. But your father . . . he wouldn't take care of you, and I had to take you along with me on the train from Philadelphia to New York. You were little and had a cold, and by the time I got there, I was so frazzled, I didn't do very well. It was the first time I didn't do well at an audition. But it broke my confidence . . . forever."

"I didn't know that."

"Water. That's water under the bridge, like they say. Let's listen to some music," my mother said. "Cecilia Bartoli. She's the greatest living soprano." She plugged a CD into the car stereo. "This is her latest, from the *opera proibita*, I want you to hear it."

"What's that?"

"It's music written in the eighteenth century, from the time the popes outlawed opera."

"I didn't know opera had ever been forbidden."

"The church thought opera could only bring sin and damnation. But composers found a way to circumvent the ban . . . by creating oratorio based on Bible stories or allegories."

"I'm thinking of canceling the trip to England," I suddenly blurted out.

"What?" she asked. "Why?"

"I don't know. It's not a good time."

"You should go."

"But I've taken too many days off from work this year—"

"Stop finding excuses. It doesn't matter. You need to do this."

"I can just send the damn postcard by certified mail. I don't really have to go."

"But you do. Don't do what I did."

"I don't understand."

"You have to follow your instincts. You can't second-guess your-self all the time. You have to act and not just sit back."

"Are you talking about me or about yourself?"

"Both."

"So why didn't you leave him? Why didn't you leave him when you found out about her?"

"I almost did . . . many times," she said, and she was quiet for a while, taking in Bartoli's voice on the CD.

"My father, Meyer . . . he was a wonderful man," my mother suddenly spoke again. "You were named for him. His name meant 'light' too. But he died too young. I know he would have loved you, Leora. You know, he had perfect pitch. He wasn't a musician or a singer himself, but he understood music. No one had an ear like him. If my father had lived, I would have been a different person. I would have had a different life. I would have been able to be stronger."

I thought of my father, the chrome pitch pipe he'd carry with him in his pants pocket. I used to think the pipe was magical, appearing and disappearing suddenly in the cup of his hand, its tiny spurt of sounds, the notes in raised lettering on the shiny disc. He'd breathe into the key, and then he'd begin, the music on the heels of that one clear note.

"The truth is . . . I'm to blame."

"What do you mean?"

"I knew it somehow, but I didn't want to believe it. I knew it on that day, and then again."

"What day?"

"That first day, when you and I landed in America, and she was there at the airport, like I told you. And then again . . . in Niagara, a few years later."

"In Niagara?"

"I should have stopped it sooner. I should never have let her into our lives. That's why I stayed with him, because I couldn't forgive myself."

"It wasn't your fault, Mom. You can't blame yourself."

"But I do," she said, enunciating each word, and I knew then that she would never be dissuaded.

We were near Venice Beach now and I could smell the ocean not far off. But suddenly I felt tired. "Do you mind if we just go back?"

"Of course I don't mind," she said, touching my cheek.

We got to her house and I fell asleep on their couch in the living room. When I woke up, I heard music playing. I thought it was the same Bartoli CD my mother had played in the car.

"Mom?"

I got up from the sofa and looked for her in the kitchen, but she wasn't there. I could smell the night air stealing in. Her bedroom door was ajar, and my mother was standing, her back turned to me. I listened to the music. The voice was enchanting, and I could almost see the costumes on the open stage, painted backdrops dripping with color, the props and the orchestra pit, a curtain rising, but I couldn't hear any instruments or any accompaniment. There was no artifice in the *a cappella* voice. It had been stripped away, leaving only vulnerability. But it wasn't the CD that was playing.

It was my mother singing.

I didn't want her to see me, and I stepped away, returning to the living room. Like the popes, she'd long banished opera from her own life. Still, she couldn't completely part with it. And I sat in her living room, listening to her voice and her secret song.

"*Come nembo che fugge col vento,*" she sang, throwing her head back, her top notes finding power. "As a cloud that flies with the wind. Stern and angry I flee from you. If deceit is all my sustenance. How can I live in truth?"

We landed in Rome one hot and muggy August, but with no clue as to where we were going to stay. It was my friend Hilda's idea we stop in Rome for a few days on our way back from Israel to the States. She said she knew some Italian, and Alitalia had a special offer for students.

Turned out she didn't really know much Italian, and we were easily duped by the taxi driver who dropped us off at the pensione he recommended. Later we discovered that the communal bathroom was down a long hallway and the shower only worked if we fed stacks of lire into the slot of an attached box.

Too hot to eat, we existed on gelati and iced espresso, making our way to the rotund Castel Sant'Angelo, Hadrian's fortress, the Coliseum, the Trevi Fountain, and up the Spanish Steps. And laughing, we two Jewish girls darted in and out of a confessional booth in a hushed Vatican. The next day, Hilda suggested we should go to Capri to get away from the heat, and a crowded train ride to Naples and a boat ride later, we spent one afternoon at the azure port, barely making it back to Naples to catch the last train to Rome, and our flight back to the States in the morning.

"What about the Teatro dell'Opera di Roma?" my mother asked when I returned home and recounted our schoolgirl adventures. "Did you see it? Did you go there? I hear it's so beautiful." And when I told her we hadn't, she sighed, and I wished I'd gone there, for her.

Twenty-five

"*Here* it is, Leora," my mother said, just as I was about to leave to go back home. She handed me a brownish envelope. Inside was one tiny square photo.

I looked closer at the photo. "It's the three of us—you, and . . . Rhea . . . and me, in between?"

It was the first time I'd said Rhea's name out loud in front of my mother in a long time, and I flinched as I said it. I thought my mother would react, but she didn't.

"I remember I was so afraid to put you up on that stone railing. I hated Niagara. It was cold and rainy, and everywhere there were bridges. Each time we came to one of those damn bridges, your father wanted to take a photo, but I was scared you might fall into the water. Rhea kept saying I was being silly. She was always interfering that way. She was always taking over and pushing me aside. You can even see it in my face, in the picture. I was so naive, so trusting of your father."

"I don't remember going to Niagara. Where is this exactly?" I asked.

"I don't know. Some bridge. *She* did all the driving on that trip. I was so tired and tried to sleep most of the time. You and I sat in the back seat, and I didn't really have a good idea where we were. We were only there for barely a day, in and out, just to go in and out of the country for our visas or something," she continued.

"Are there other photos?"

"Yes," she said, and she went over to a file cabinet in the hallway and pulled out a photo album. There was one of the four of us in a horse-drawn Niagara tour carriage, and another of my father standing in front of the Niagara Parks Commission building. The last was one of me again, sitting on the bridge, this time between my father and Rhea, and it sent a shiver up my spine. It was my mother who must have taken the photo, my young mother, barely a year and a half in America, snapping a photo of this strange trio, her husband, her only child, and Rhea.

"Why are you showing this to me now?"

"Because I wanted you to see it. All these years I think I was ashamed, about how I let her barge into our lives and take over, but now I know it's important for you to have it. The photo will tell you what you need to know. You have to go to London with Talia, Leora. Take your daughter and spend time with her like you planned. Talk to her. Talk to her about everything. I should have done that. I should have taken you on trips. I should have talked to you about love and sex. We should have gone together to beautiful places. You know, when you left for Israel, and we took you to the airport in New York, I tried to be strong, but when you disappeared among the other passengers, Ron, who was only seven at the time, said, 'She will never come back to live with us again,' and then it hit me, he was right, and I cried. I should have talked to you more. And I should have prepared you better for life. Don't let anything keep you from this trip. There was a reason you found the postcard. It was meant to be," she said. She looked relieved to have said it all at once, all her misgivings stitched together as though one whole quilt of regret.

"I'm not so sure about that. Not sure that anything is meant to be. It's all just chance."

"No," she pronounced with absolute assurance. "There was a reason for you to find your Maynard."

"Mom, he's not *my* Maynard."

"But he is," she insisted. "I looked it up. Did you know 'Maynard' is a French and German word, a combination. The French word is *mainard*, and it means strength."

"Strength?"

"I think you are finding your strength by trying to find this Maynard person."

"I'm not sure about that."

My parents' porch light sensor suddenly came on with a tiny flicker.

"I don't feel courageous at all."

"But tell me that you'll go?"

"I don't know."

I thought about the months I'd spent researching the postcard and the British private on the internet; the people I'd written emails to and corresponded with all over England, Australia, and Brooklyn; the archives, libraries, and museums I'd contacted; the trip to London I'd booked months before I was even close to finding Maynard. I'd thought it was Rhea who had started me and kept me on this journey, certain that it was Rhea's irrepressible spirit, her way of defying all conventions. But now I realized it was someone else whose hand had touched my shoulder. It was my mother.

And I still didn't know if I would go.

Twenty-six

The house was dark when I came back home, and I turned on the lamp on my desk. I took out the photo my mother had given me and looked at it more closely. Like an old postcard, the photo had a white border, the irregular ends serrated, as though they were protecting the tiny, three-inch boundaries of the image and its limitations. But there was something wrong in the perfect square frame, as though it was covering up the chaos. I could feel it even in its proportions, its geometry, the unnatural black and white. On the back, in the left-hand corner, the words "Niagara Falls" were written in my father's edgy handwriting. In ink, never pencil, the photos he took were always marked in this way, encapsulated and titled. Next to the words was a careful inked date stamp, OCT 18, 1957, as if by marking the time and place, he could somehow tame the photograph he'd taken as he stood across from the trio.

The photo was of me sitting balanced on the edge of the stone balustrade of a bridge between my mother and Rhea. Both wore long A-line coats, the river cold and misty behind them. The bridge too seemed to reach backward into an icy path. To the right, another span, lower, was closer to the water, and I wasn't sure whether it was real or the first bridge's shadow. Rhea wore gloves, my mother was bare-handed. Both held on to me, as though we were all fused together.

My mother was smiling and had her hand on my knee. Rhea only eyed the lens, her silk scarf tied and fixed, and it seemed determined against her chin.

I was smiling too, my hands folded politely on my lap. I held on to something long and thin, maybe a stick or a branch I'd found. I sat up straight with only my ankles crossed, my winter coat buttons bright, the woolen jacket stretched tightly across my tiny chest, but one button was missing. I wore white anklet socks and shiny, patent leather shoes, and a tweedy hat that matched my coat. Pressed together, we were three, and there was only the photograph to remember the journey to and from Niagara, the water and stone bridges, crossed and uncrossed. I didn't remember.

I was about to put the photograph away when I noticed something else, my father's mistake. Hurrying to take the photo, to memorialize the moment, he'd forgotten the lamppost behind the women, an amateur photographer's mistake, and it barged into the frame of the photograph, flat and two-dimensional, making it seem as if the lamp was growing out of my head. But when I looked at the photo again, it almost seemed as if it wasn't an oversight, as though the lamppost itself had taken pity on me. It stretched and grabbed up into the gray sky for me. The top of the lamppost reached up far beyond the photo, further than its thin, paper borders, far beyond my little girl's hat, and it was there, like a thunderbolt, a way for me to follow the sound of the light.

Suddenly, I wanted to know exactly where the bridge was and where the photo was taken. I Googled the keywords "Niagara bridges" and came up with hundreds of websites related to the falls. I clicked on a few, and photos of the falls faded in and out on my screen in syncopated flash animations.

I scrolled down and found a site entirely devoted to the bridges in and around the falls, and I learned there were six existing bridges. I read about each of their histories, as well as the ones that had collapsed prior to my mother's photo, in 1889 and 1938. There were suspension bridges and cantilevered spans, others with railroad tracks and giant metal arches. I looked at the images on the web closely, comparing them to the photograph, but I couldn't make out if any of them were the same bridge.

Then I scanned the 3½" x 3½" photo into my computer and enlarged it a hundred percent. I pored over the lines in the pavement, the stones of the bridge, the faded, dwindling backdrop of trees. There were no cars on the road, and in the distance, only the faint outline of something that looked like a gabled estate. Was it the old Oak Hall estate I'd seen on the internet, or was it my imagination? Every stone, every line in the photograph seemed to be a part of me, but there were no road signs, no landmarks I could make out.

The bridge could be anywhere.

I emailed the website host, describing the bridge as best I could, explaining it looked like one used by both pedestrians and cars, and lined with lampposts.

He responded and asked me if it was single level or multiple. Did it have a big steel arch or multiple concrete arches?

I emailed him back, this time attaching a copy of my photo. Could it be the Peace Bridge crossing the Niagara between Buffalo and Fort Erie, erected in 1927, I asked him. Or was it the Rainbow Bridge, built in 1940?

No, he answered the next morning. It wasn't any of the major bridges across the Niagara River, but it might be the bridge that crossed the forebay of the Canadian Power Company about one hundred yards upriver from the Horseshoe Falls, he said.

The roadway is the Niagara Parkway and is located within the confines of Queen Victoria Park. You can see the mist from the Horseshoe Falls rising in the lower right corner of the picture. And the bridge has no name.

I went back online and found only one photo of the bridge in the Niagara Falls Public Library collection. It was an old, black-and-white photograph from an unknown date, taken from a different angle than my mother's photograph, but it appeared to be the same bridge. There were cranes and building equipment nearby, scraps of wood and metal scattered in the foreground, and it was hard to tell whether the bridge was in a state of assemblage or deconstruction.

On another Niagara website, I clicked on to a "Listen to the Falls" link, and the crash of the water siphoning through my computer sounded hollow, just white noise. On the same site, several "falls-cams" were offered to viewers, one with a panoramic and zoom lens, another with a pan/tilt that allowed for a 360-degree rotation, all from the rooftop of a hotel. But the last webcam, named "Edge of the Falls," was most intriguing. In a purple haze, shadowy figures appeared and disappeared in a cloudy twilight, walking up to the railing, the water below almost unrecognizable except for a faint flicker of movement. A freak spring snowstorm had left small tufts of snow on the guardrail. I couldn't stop watching the eerie scene, the curve of the railing and then a sharp, angular turn.

People gravitated toward the guardrail, then moved away, and returned. They came in pairs and threesomes, others alone, only their outlines. They seemed to me on the brink, the rim of the world, and I conjured up the falls unseen to the right of the people in the livestream. They didn't stand still for very long, and only stood, it seemed, to pose for a photo. Every once in a while, I could make out an arm or someone leaning over the railing, and I held my breath. All of a sudden, the sky must have brightened, because I could see a tiny burst of color in someone's jacket.

"I'll go," I said out loud, and somehow I knew my mother heard me even though she was in her own house on the other side of the Santa Monica Mountain range. She was awake, unable to sleep, naming all the people in her elementary school class, I was sure, waiting for my answer.

I was still watching the fuzzy webcam when near the railing, one person became two. They separated, but then like lovers, they soon seemed to melt into one another, forming one being.

Someone knocked, and I opened the door of my student apartment in the Rehavia section of Jerusalem. He stood at the landing, one arm hanging loosely over the shoulder of a girl. I didn't know either of them. He was coming to see my roommate, Neal, he said, grinning from ear to ear, his polo shirt collar neat. I looked very hard, but I didn't find any camouflage, any concealments in the smile. His name was David, and I was sure the girl by his side was his girlfriend, but I was wrong.

A couple of months later, we had a first date. I thought he'd run away fast when I asked him to drive me to a Romanian bookstore in Tel Aviv so I could buy some hard-to-find romance novels to send back to my grandmother in the States. But he didn't.

Later, we met up with my roommates for a party in Tel Aviv, and he drove us all back to Jerusalem in his father's two-seater Peugeot. Bright orange, the car seemed as though it lit up its own way across the darkened streets. And even though my roommates sat crammed behind us, in the cool night there was only the old, winding road to Jerusalem, the white of its ancient stones ahead of us, and the way he traced my fingertips with his own as they melted into mine.

Twenty-seven

In late June, David and I came to say goodbye to my parents. It was the Thursday evening before we were to leave. My father greeted us at the door and ushered us into the living room. I could smell the cinnamon raisin noodle kugel my mother was baking in the oven for Friday night Shabbat dinner.

My mother came in from the kitchen and sat across from us on the sofa. "So, you'll call me from New York?"

"Of course I will."

"And when you land in London?"

"Of course."

"I looked at the weather report for New York and London. You shouldn't have too much rain, but make sure to take an umbrella. Oh, and remember, there's an eight-hour time difference between Los Angeles and London," she continued.

I smiled. I was sure she would also check with the airlines for our departure and arrival times and look out for any flight changes.

My father sat quietly on one of two velvety chairs near the piano. He knew about the purpose of this trip, had overheard many of the conversations I'd had with my mother about it, but had never asked me anything about it.

"So, what do you think about all this?" I asked him.

"All this trouble you went to . . . for a little postcard," he said. "Maybe when you come back you can put my thesis into a book?" It was his master's thesis about the origins of Hasidic music, a typed copy of which he'd given me months ago.

"Sure, sure," I said, but I knew somehow I wouldn't get to it.

We then talked a little about London and the time we were all there, my mother remembering almost every detail of that one family trip we took together, my father remembering little.

"My favorite part was the gardens of Windsor Castle," my mother said.

"Mine too."

"It's good to be the Queen of England . . . and to be rich," my mother said.

Then she showed us the videos Ron had taken on their trip together to Israel and Bucharest a couple of months back, in April. In one video, a group of balladeers in Romanian peasant costumes serenaded my father in a Bucharest café on his eighty-third birthday. Their accordions tilted left and right and he smiled like a schoolboy, thanking them in his mother tongue. Ron had zoomed in on his face and I could see the memories, both bitter and sweet, behind his eyes.

"Did you see your old apartment in Bucharest? Where you used to live with your parents?" I asked my father.

"No," my mother piped in. "The entire block was knocked down by the Communists."

"That's a shame," I said.

"No, better not to have seen it," he sighed.

"Really?" I asked.

"What's the point?"

Later, my mother gave me a hug, said goodbye, and left to attend to the kugel in the oven. My father accompanied us to the entrance foyer.

"Love you," I said, as I kissed him on the cheek. He saw I was waiting for him to respond in kind.

"I'm sorry. I cannot say it," he said, haltingly, shaking his head.

I stiffened. "You can't say 'love you'? Really?"

"I don't know, I just can't."

I closed my eyes. The rectangular foyer seemed to close in on me, and the mirror, the Persian rug, even the table where my parents left their keys in a little dish all felt suffocating.

I grabbed David's arm. "Let's just go. And now, please." I started out the door. "What kind of a father can't say I love you to his daughter?" I said loud enough for my father to hear.

"Yes, let's go," David said. "Let's go now." He took my hand and pulled me out just past the screen door.

"Wait," my father said.

I turned around. "What now?"

"Let's just go now," David repeated.

"No." I stopped and came back into the foyer. "You know what? It's actually about time I said it."

"Said what?" my father asked, but I could see he immediately regretted asking the question.

Ever since my mother had given me the Niagara photo, the picture of the three of us, my mother, me, and Rhea, that photo with its seemingly ordinary image masking its true meaning, it had lit a slow burn fire in my gut. But his words had thrown gasoline on that fire.

I'm sorry I cannot say it.

I erupted. "What hurts me the most, even more than you not being able to say ' I love you,' is that you brought Rhea into our lives. You didn't keep her apart from us. You could have at least done that for us. You brought her in, and you kept her in. You let her do things for all of us, for me and for Ron. You let me love her. You shouldn't have done that. And Mom wants me to unlove her, for all of us to unlove her and Dena, and I want to, for Mom's sake, but I can't. You put me in between all of you. Why did you do that? Why?" I asked, my hands shaking.

My father looked at me but didn't answer. The three of us stood there for a moment, no one speaking, my "why?" left hanging in the air, and then he did something I didn't remember him ever doing. He reached out to button up my jacket, as though I was five years old. And with that, he repeated the Yiddish phrase he always invoked before any of us took a trip. "*Gey gezuntereit und com gezuntereit.*" Go in good health, and come back in good health.

"Time for us to go," David said.

It had been a long and exhausting pre-wedding week of misunderstandings and miscues between families. But when he caught sight of me in the lobby of the synagogue, David took my hand and motioned everyone away. "We need a moment to ourselves," he announced, and he reached for the nearest door. It turned out to be a broom closet.

The closet was small and smelled of bleach and wax. We stood inches apart from one another, our wedding minutes away, the guests already seated for the ceremony, but we lingered. Only one dim light bulb illuminated the tiny space filled with buckets, mops, and sponges, but it was as if we'd left everyone behind and had suddenly run away and eloped. We giggled.

"It's just us," he said, his sweet breath on my cheek. "Just us," he repeated. "But now it's time to go," he continued, and the dragonfly on his tie caught a splinter of light from nowhere, and my layers of white chiffon whispered yes in our cocoon of brooms and light.

Twenty-eight

The four of us flew to New York. The plan was after spending a few days together in New York, David and Oren would return to Los Angeles, and Talia and I would continue on to London. When we landed at JFK, I was excited. I was now a little less than halfway to London, I told myself. The next evening, we all went to a magic show at the Lyceum Theater, the city warm, noisy, and teeming with people. Across the street from our hotel, there was a wall of open windows blowing their curtains out into the street, and ACs whirring everywhere. The following day, David and I met up with friends and headed out to Brooklyn and found the apartment where Caldwell lived on Clinton Avenue; then we took a bus to Green-Wood Cemetery to see where he and his wife were buried.

In the taxi to the airport a few days later, Talia and I started saying our goodbyes to David and Oren, and I suddenly realized it would be the first time in years that I would be on a long trip without David. I would be on my own with my teenage daughter, and I would have to rely only on myself for the end of this crazy mission. I started fidgeting in the taxi.

Oren looked at me and gave me a hug. "Don't worry, Mom. Everything will be okay," he said.

"Sure, sure, of course. Everything will be okay," I echoed. Oren and David then left to go to their domestic terminal, but when Talia and I got to our check-in desk, we were told our London-bound plane would be delayed for a full twenty-four hours.

Twenty-four hours? My heart sank.

We were bused to a dreary Airport Radisson that was surrounded by a lattice of tiny houses and yards. Straddling Jamaica and Howard beaches on Jamaica Bay, it seemed like any other suburban New York neighborhood except it was dwarfed by the vastness of JFK. For an hour, I slogged up and down the airless hotel elevator, trying out various rooms and key cards until I found a room with a workable AC. A tired-looking buffet in the lounge sent us back to the room where we ordered room service, and Talia watched Wimbledon on TV, the view of the lawn-green tennis court, its rectangle offering a small respite.

The tennis balls lobbed back and forth on the TV screen, and with every smack of the ball, another doubt crept in. For so long I'd been the working mom and wife, always responsible, playing it safe, always careful, prepared, never without an emergency Tylenol, Band-Aids, and Tic Tacs in my handbag. Other people did weird, adventurous things; not me.

"Maybe we should just take the next plane home to Los Angeles?" I asked Talia.

"Come on, Mom," Talia said, coming out of the small, windowless bathroom. "You can do this. We can do this."

"Sure we can," I said, trying hard to sound positive.

"Oh, my God," Talia suddenly yelled out, jumping up and down and clapping. "Maria Sharapova just defeated defending champion Serena Williams. Can you believe this? It's a huge upset!" she cried out. "No one thought she could do it. I bet she didn't even think she could do it."

And then I remembered that once not-so-careful me who had ridden on the back seat of a Vespa down hairpin turns on the hills of Jerusalem and had slept under the stars on *Ras Mohammed* beach in the Sinai desert. Maybe that me wasn't completely gone.

"Okay," I said. "We can do this."

The next morning, we were up before dawn to catch the plane to London. Seven hours later, Heathrow, undergoing renovation, was a maze of dark corridors. Ceilings sagged, and tarps covered up equipment and abandoned counters. Arrows pointed to more hallways and stairs. It was early Sunday, but still, there were masses of people, families wielding luggage carts everywhere. Outside, the air was muggy, and we stood in a long line to catch a black cab to the city. The cabbie drove fast, but it seemed as if we were barely moving, and from the left side of the road, the streets seemed askew, the city inscrutable and tomb-like.

The taxi let us off at Chesham Place, an angled corner of apartments and smaller embassies. Our building was once a private townhouse, but the five-story building, painted pastel yellow, had been converted into short-term rental apartments. There was no key waiting for us at the hotel across the street from our apartment as promised, but a young concierge took pity on us, making tea and toast while we waited. Finally, someone came by and brought me the key to the apartment, but exhausted, I couldn't see its charm. At first glance, I only saw the small leak in the kitchen, and mangled blinds in the living room.

"Ten days seem like such a long time to stay . . . here, doesn't it?" Talia said, looking around, and I nodded, unpacking little.

"Maybe I should have booked a shorter trip," I said, wondering if I could change the reservations.

"Stop, Mom. Really?"

"Stopping. I'm just jet-lagged."

Talia went to bed and dozed off, but I couldn't fall asleep. Pacing around the flat, I wished I'd brought my laptop with me. The rental agency had written ahead of time that there was no internet access, and I'd grudgingly left it at home.

Finally, I went back to bed and fell asleep until a brilliant, northerly light hit the blinds, insistent, claiming the bedroom window at four in the morning. I pulled up the blinds. Chesham Place was all white. Pont Street offered orange-and-white buildings, black wrought iron, pots of flowers, and the green of a small triangle of park. The bedroom overlooked an old mews where horses and carriages once rattled over its uneven cobblestone. I moved on to the kitchen window. It had a view of an intersection, vans coming to make their deliveries.

A light rain tapped on the window and down below umbrellas opened up. Talia slept, and I unpacked, left her a note, and went out to find a supermarket. On the street, there was more color, red buses, shiny black cabs, and canary-yellow license plates. I bought a *Herald Tribune* from a newspaper stand and returned with two armloads of food from Waitrose market—freshly baked bread and jam, butter and honey, eggs and fruits. I wanted to fill up all the counters of the tiny kitchen, and I started to make breakfast, but Talia was still asleep, and I watched her.

Across the bed, my daughter was a gift, wrapped in cotton linen, so precious.

"Take your daughter and spend time with her. Talk to her," my mother had said.

I sat down on the bed and whispered to Talia. "I'm so happy you're here with me," I said, planting a light kiss on her forehead, and she stirred.

"I'm happy too," she yawned, settling into my arm.

We ate breakfast together, spreading out on the sofa of the living room. We were both still jet-lagged and decided not to go out yet, watching reruns of *Charmed* on TV. Later, we walked around, taking in the noises of the city. Knightsbridge station was close by, but unlike the New York subway, which was noisy even aboveground, the Underground lay stories beneath the ground, quiet, barely a shush on the street. When we returned to the apartment, I called Tom in

Stibbard to tell him we would visit him soon. He was excited. I started to get excited too.

A few days later, the steep, narrow staircase and the blue-and-white carpeting to the third-floor flat seemed completely familiar and no longer cramped. There was no extravagance of space here, no wasted corners, and it sucked me in close, a closeness I hadn't felt before. Chesham Place was a triangle of roads forming the periphery of a garden.

One afternoon, we walked around the garden but could only find one entrance, a wrought iron gate with an overgrown, narrow path to the inside, and only a stone urn barely visible through the gate. The sign warned PRIVATE GARDENS, beckoning like a secret as we tried to push open the locked gate. When we asked at the hotel across the street, the bellman gave us a little history about the area, telling us that the garden had been laid out in 1831, originally part of the Lowndes estate, but it was only available to key holders.

"Any chance to get a key for an hour?" I asked.

"I'm afraid not, ma'am. We here all call it the secret love triangle garden." He laughed. "I've never seen the gate open."

Talia and I continued to walk toward Hyde Park, following the path of Serpentine Lake, and each park bench seemed to be an invitation to sit. The way to Buckingham Palace was lined with plane trees known for their khaki camouflage-patterned bark of mottled gray, olive, and cream. We walked for hours, the map of London I'd brought with me starting to wear out, and I put it away, letting only my camera be our guide.

It was late October, and Paris was dark and rainy when David and I landed at Charles de Gaulle airport. I was battling a bout of vertigo, and it took us a few weeks to find and settle into a ground-floor apartment that overlooked noisy Boulevard Vaugirard. Our landlord, an eccentric artist born in Cairo, lived in his atelier above us. Superstitious, he'd scold us from his window if we left an open umbrella to dry near the doorway of the building and complain of our other offenses by yelling through some strange voice pipe with a funnel-shaped horn he'd jury-rigged between his apartment and our bathroom.

A couple of months later, we escaped him to a fourth-floor apartment in the center of the city, near the Palais Royale with a glimpse of the Eiffel tower from our bedroom window. David went to work for an acquaintance of his father, and I enrolled in the Alliance Française on the Boulevard Raspail to learn French. In between classes, I drank up cups of dark espresso and lit up unfiltered cigarettes with the rest of my international classmates, all of us trying hard to act French. In the afternoons I was on my own. I'd found David's old camera in the trunk we'd shipped, and taught myself photography from a Time–Life book series. The camera took me past the gravelly paths of the Tuileries, the rows of trees along the Champs Élysées, the bridges and banks of the Seine, and the crooked streets of Le Marais. In an old drawer I found a key to the small, locked storeroom that was once the original kitchen, and made it into a makeshift darkroom. And at night, I closed the door, surrounded by the magic of three trays and the reddish glow of the darkroom bulb.

Twenty-nine

After three days in London without my computer, I was having a bad case of internet withdrawal. I asked around for an internet café and found the Easyinternetcafé on Oxford Street. It was hardly noticeable near a tourist kiosk selling Union Jack T-shirts and hidden on the top floor of a crowded Subway sandwich restaurant. Up the crooked stairs, I almost collided with a couple of backpackers, but for three pounds, I bought an orange-and-white ticket from a machine that allowed me to surf the net for an hour. Rows of wooden cubicles ran across the room, each equipped with a computer and a small stool, and I sat down.

"Are you writing home?" a friendly voice said from above. He had a couple of cameras and set them down on the table of the adjoining cubicle.

"No, I guess this is home for now," I said.

"Funny how that happens," he mused. "Have you figured out how to work this thing?" he asked, and I showed him how to use the token and log on.

On the way back to the flat, I noticed the gate to the private garden was unlocked and I took a peek inside at the triangle of grass edged with flowers and shrubbery, and for a few minutes it was just mine.

When I returned, Talia was getting dressed.

"What took you so long?" she asked, pinning her hair up.

"I was getting my email, and I got a peek inside that private garden."

"Good for you! I was thinking . . . I don't want to be just a tourist here," Talia announced.

"Me neither." I promised her we'd stay clear of the tourist traps, and for the next couple days we walked only as far as our legs could take us, up and down the same streets until they became ours, washing laundry together in sweet-smelling soap, folding clothes, as though we'd never lived anywhere else.

Finally, one morning, we succumbed to the lure of the hop-on, hop-off buses and walked to Victoria Station to catch a tour. It was cold and windy, but we both chose the last row of the top of the double-decker, even with a storm brewing, and settled in.

From the top deck, I could see the ubiquitous security cameras everywhere, perched on buildings and on poles, roving eyes in all directions, and I too felt as though I'd been given an extra pair of eyes. The sky seemed to open up to the spires, following the arc and spokes of the shiny London Eye. The bus route was narrow, the bus driver often coming within inches of vehicles in the opposite direction, and the medieval buildings too abutted slender and hard, one up against the other.

When we got off, I called my mother.

"You sound good," she said.

"I am. We're good."

"I'm happy for you. Call me tomorrow at the same time."

"I will."

Later in the day, we took the Underground to Green Park. Inside the cylinder of the station, the train approached, and car doors opened quickly. We held on to bright yellow poles and then found seats along the tartan-patterned benches, all facing inward instead of the direction of the train. I remembered the ghost stations I'd read about on the internet, the ones scattered along the Underground's hundreds of miles of track. There were almost forty stations that had been abandoned over the years, and where the trains never stopped anymore. Some of the platforms had been bricked up and used during World War II, converted into shelters or operations centers. I looked out the train window, and for a moment I thought I could make out the blur of green-and-tan tiles, a phantom station at Brompton Road.

Still cold the next day, we found a Lebanese restaurant tucked above the street on the second floor. Up a narrow staircase, we sat down and feasted on heaping plates of chopped parsley, mint salads, and falafel below a greenhouse ceiling. We each ate two bowls of steaming lentil soup served by a young Russian waitress.

"Shouldn't we go see Tom by now, Mom? When are we going to visit him?" Talia asked, warmed now by the soup.

"Soon."

"But when?" she asked, picking from my plate of hummus and pita bread.

"In the next couple of days," I answered. "I'm not just ready to see him yet."

"Not ready to give up that postcard?" She laughed.

"Maybe you're right. Maybe I just want to hang on to it for another day or so."

Later, we passed a fountain, a statute of Venus bending down, a trail of water leaving her upturned hand. Nearby, on a street marked with zigzagging white lines, was the block-long Peter Jones store, built in the 1930s, the exterior wrapped in a smooth curtain-like curve of glass and steel. It was underneath its generous awning that I spotted the post office across the street, on Kings Road, only steps away. The red and yellow oval sign was small, and the storefront looked older than the other more fashionable stores lining the street. And although it was nowhere near working-class South Tottenham where Maynard had mailed the postcard, it urged me in somehow.

We crossed the street, and Talia waited outside while I went in through the wooden door. It was a small space, bulletins tacked on to the walls, a line of seven or eight people ahead, and I took my place at the end. Four clerks sat behind glass, like tellers in a bank, looking down, then up as each patron approached.

"Can I help you?" the clerk asked when it was my turn at the window, her badge sitting crisply on her blue vest, and I asked for two stamps. "First class or second?" she asked.

"Just two, one-penny stamps, please."

I knew it was a strange request, but she detached the stamps from a larger sheet and handed them to me. Instead of the two profiles of King George VI in diluted red that I'd found on the postcard, they were deep purple, with a likeness of his successor, his daughter, a young Queen Elizabeth.

"You can't even mail a postcard for two p," the clerk said with a laugh and looked up at me.

"I know." I smiled back, slipping the stamps into my purse.

"Mom?" Talia poked her head inside the post office. "Let's go home, please?"

"Home? You mean to Los Angeles?"

"No, Mom. Home here, to our apartment on Chesham Place."

Our third flat in Paris overlooked the elegant Avenue Mozart in the 16th and was only steps from the Jasmin Metro station, named after the French poet, Jacques Jasmin. Built in the mid-1800s, the facade showed off busts of Mozart himself, but our bedroom walls were covered in shocking pink satin, the living room in bordello burgundy. David said he was sure someone looking for the previous "madam" tenant would knock on our door late one night, but it too soon became home.

The floor plan was unusual, a skylit closet that doubled as a second bedroom, which became a favorite stopover for college friends traveling in Europe, and the one bathroom that could only be reached through the dining room. But the large salon windows opened up with a view to the symmetry of the streets below.

We bought a used olive-green Fiat and on weekends drove up north to Brussels, Bruges, and Amsterdam, south to the Loire, to Mont-Saint-Michel on the western coast of France, and east to Munich, where my mother's sister lived.

A year later, we moved to the south of France, to the tiny port town of Saint-Tropez where David managed a small boutique on its main artery, the Rue Gambetta. We arrived there sometime in May, a month before the summer crowds, and before most of the glamorous yachts docked and the summer discos opened. May was still a time to take in the charm of old Saint-Tropez, its annual patron saint parade, and the old cemetery of brilliant white tombstones overlooking the Mediterranean. There, home became a second-story apartment above a biker café, the Vespas and motorcycles beneath us revving their engines into the night.

On the rainy day we left Europe to return to the States, we took the train to the airport. Station stops melted away as the train made its way northward, until we passed Drancy, the name flying by in a blur. But I felt a sudden chill as I remembered. Drancy station had served as an assembly and detention camp for French Jews on their way to extermination. And in spite of all the beauty and grace two years in France had given me, I was happy to say goodbye.

Thirty

Liverpool station was a mix of old and new—Victorian brick-work and Bath stone, a weblike ceiling, melding blue cast iron and acanthus leaf. Two towers presided over the contemporary Liverpool Street entrance, and shiny stairs led down to the main concourse encircled with a balcony of shops. There was a distinct sound to the concourse, its zigzag of people, the hum of McDonald's and cash machines. Like a loud murmur, it rose and fell with the train departure announcements over the loudspeaker system. The station was mostly full of local commuters, but trains also connected to the seaports of the North and Baltic Seas.

Our nine o'clock train to Norwich felt like a womb, mostly empty at that hour, rumbling away from the city, dark in the warren of tunnels rattling northward from the station. In the brick tunnels, there was a range of colors—mossy green and orange-yellow, then tan darkened by the black soot of the rails. After the tunnels, we passed the small station at Manningtree, then on through the Stour Valley where countryside of horses and sheep emerged outside the window. We stretched out onto four seats, and Talia and I both fell asleep, as if sleep was a new magic we'd conjured together.

When I woke up, I noticed a woman who looked like a London lawyer preparing for a trial. I watched her, poring over her legal brief, highlighting passages, and I was happy to be far away from briefs and lawyers and courthouses. We arrived at Norwich station almost two hours later. Finding a cab, we left the station's Italianate clock tower and arched facade and the River Wensum behind.

We dropped our luggage off in the room of our hotel, which was attached to a golf course. An hour later Tom and Winnie met us outside our hotel, their silhouettes inexplicably recognizable on the graveled pathway as we came out to greet them. Tom was slight, Winnie tinier still, but their steel-blue eyes had not faded with age. I wondered for a minute whether I should shake hands or hug, but Tom didn't hesitate. He greeted me with open arms.

Talia and I then climbed into the back seat of Tom's silvery car, like children newly adopted by a kind family. Tom drove, Winnie by his side, taking us into the heart of Norfolk. Clouds mixed with rain on the ride there, a kaleidoscope of light and dark. We stopped in the village of Reepham, barely a slip of a town, for something to eat, but it was too late for lunch at an old brewery house hotel, and we could only take a quick look inside the Georgian building, finding our way through the dark lobby to the original wood staircase and paneling. Hungry, we settled in some canvas chairs in front of a grocery on the main square, only steps away from the town church, biting into freshly baked savory pies. Across the street, there was still a narrow doorway where coaches once entered. We got back into Tom's car, and as he drove, he began to tell us about himself and the family.

"I was born in 1922, the youngest of a family of eight children. We all lived in a rented, terraced house in North London, the house being shared by two families, one living upstairs and one downstairs. I don't remember much about my early childhood other than being taken by my mother to a small timber-clad hall used by the London City Mission for Christian worship. Occasionally, Mum took me to an outing at the seaside for the day. During the journey by an open, single-deck bus, gospel hymns were sung. It was my mother's one joy, singing that is, something that took her away from her difficult life."

"Yes," Winnie added. "She belonged to a chapel choir, and they'd go around singing in hospitals. She loved to sing," she said, and I thought of my mother. "After the war, I moved to Ontario, Canada, finding a life there for myself. I said goodbye to my family at home rather than the railway station. Alone in the compartment, and watching the other families say farewell, though, I wished I'd let my brothers come with me to the station."

"What happened then?" Talia asked.

"A group of us sailed to Canada, docking at New Brunswick. We boarded a train for Toronto, and later on I made my way to Tilsonburg, a small town in the tobacco-growing region of Southern Ontario. It was in this town that my aunt Charlotte lived with her husband and son. I stayed with my aunt for a while, and then moved on to a YMCA where I was discovered by a choirmaster who gave me singing lessons and taught me to read music."

We arrived at Tom's cottage of pale, yellow brick, his garden bursting with early summer flowers, and with an overgrown but benevolent neglect.

"What's the exact street address here?" I asked, wanting to write it down.

"No street address." Tom smiled. "Just a name—Little Gables."

"Little Gables," I repeated. The name was perfect, and I thought about all the names of the grand houses I'd passed through in my childhood—Dragon Hill, Ivy Hall, Linden Drake. And this was no grand estate. It was better, just a simple cottage out of a storybook.

In the living room, the walls were a peach pink, alive with the sounds of a mantel clock ticking. We sat in his kitchen, at a rough pine table, drinking hot tea and eating biscuits from a tin. The house was quiet, and there were only the sounds of a distant thunder and of the squirrels and finches feasting on a feeder outside. Talia was at the head of the table, videotaping our strange reunion. The video camera looked natural in her steady hand, and the afternoon melted with a light rain.

"Here are some photographs of Arthur and our family," Winnie said, opening a photo album she'd prepared. Winnie was in her mid-eighties, but still girlish in a pink polo shirt, sweet as the sugar pot she offered us with our tea, easy to imagine as the only sister in a household of brothers. One photo showed Winnie, maybe five years old, holding an even younger Tom's hand.

"That photo really tells the story. We were always together, Win and me, even after all these years," Tom said, looking at his sister. "Our father was a maintenance man, doing odd jobs, sometimes cleaning houses. But there were some desperate times. We'd collect wooden boxes or barrels and split them just to earn some money."

"I remember we even talked about going to a workhouse," Winnie added. "Mum did housework for some people in Stamford Hill, a Mrs. Philips. It was really a sad life, though. Our grandmother made us call her 'Aunt Ginny,' because our mother was born out of wedlock. Poor mum. She never knew her father and always wanted to know who he was, but 'Aunt Ginny' wouldn't tell her."

"Mum's name was Harriet Delatorre Reeves," Tom said.

"But we've never figured out where the Delatorre comes from," Winnie added.

"We were so poor, three boys to a bed. I used to feel smothered by my brothers," Tom spoke up. "My happiest times were when I was in the army. I volunteered at seventeen and was assigned to the Royal Artillery. I was sent to France, Germany, and Holland, but I don't even think of them as rough times. I had lots of friends. I felt sorry for the boys who had grown up in wealth. It was hardest on them. For me, the army was where I got an education."

"That's Arthur," Winnie said, pointing to one of the snapshots.

"Where was Arthur during the war?" I asked.

"He never ended up going abroad. He had stomach ulcers and was discharged after some time," Tom clarified. "I was still in Canada when he passed away in the sixties."

After our second cup of tea, I knew it was time. I dug into my backpack to take out the postcard.

Should I say something?

"Here it is," was all I could muster. I wanted to say more—that it had been in my safekeeping for almost a year, and now I was returning it to where it should be, but all that seemed insignificant now, and I gave Tom the postcard, which I'd put in a clear plastic sleeve.

"So this is it," Tom said, turning it over. In my first email to him, I'd only sent him a copy of the side where Arthur had written his thank you. It was the first time he would see the front. Tom looked at it for a moment, then handed it to Winnie. "Such a small thing, isn't it?" he said. Then he turned to Winnie.

"Look, Win. It's addressed to someone named W. Caldwell in New York. Didn't Arthur once tell us about someone he corresponded to in New York after the war? Arthur said they would write each other about art and music."

"That's right," Winnie said.

"Once I saw a stack of letters on his desk," Tom continued. They were all tied up with string, but one was open. All I could see was that it was signed W, but I could tell Arthur didn't want me to see it. He pushed it away to the side."

W? But before I could ask, Tom put the postcard down on the table, left the room, and came back a minute later with a cardboard box.

"These are some of the letters Arthur wrote to me when I lived in Canada, and all his artwork," Tom explained, and took out some watercolors and put them on the kitchen table.

"They're beautiful," Talia exclaimed.

Arthur's watercolors were pretty, still bright after more than half a century.

"I'd love to have copies of these," I said.

"Here, take everything back with you to the States," Tom said, handing me the box. "You can photocopy them and mail them back to me."

"Are you sure? They must be so precious to you, and you barely know me."

"But I do know you," Tom insisted. "You are the person who came all the way here . . . just to return a postcard."

We were a newly formed family around Tom's kitchen table— Tom and Winnie, Talia and me, a family patched together, and I saw another family in my head, my parents and grandparents, and Rhea pulling up her chair to our cherry-red dining room table. Sometimes strangers and even interlopers had a place at the family table.

Back at our hotel, rain fell on the sixteenth-century facade of an old country manor reinvented into a Marriott, concealing its American-style interior. The ancient oak-lined driveway was swallowed up by the hotel's newly landscaped golf course. Talia went down to the lobby for hot chocolate, and I sat on the edge of the bed, Arthur's letters and photos spread out like freshly ironed linen on top of the flowery bedcover. Winnie had made copies of family photos, and I studied the grainy, black-and-white faces—Arthur and his brothers, skinny, with boyish smiles, trying to look manly, cross armed on a reedy river bank, with their black-and-white mutt. There was another of a family outing in 1928, bicycles on a country road. My favorite was a threesome: Tom in a shiny Sunday suit, grinning between Winnie and his mother, Harriet. Winnie was stylish in a bob, a worn brick building in the background, and a frilly curtain hung on a string in a window.

I read all of Arthur's letters Tom had saved. They were in stark contrast to his colorful and cheery watercolors. They were on lined, onionskin paper, thin and transparent, the same precise calligraphy, like typeset. Arthur wrote about his aunt Charlotte, and brother Bill, quoted poems, and railed against the postwar party of Winston Churchill. He described the plots of the latest movies in minute detail, and a family Christmas party. For months, it seemed, he was trying to save money to join Tom and start a new life in Canada, but nothing materialized, his paints and books his only respite from the drudgery of a string of blue-collar jobs. There was no mention of friends except for one letter where he wrote he was hoping to go to New York too, *to see the Great White Way.*

I went to sleep with Arthur's words buzzing in my head.

I've drawn on my wages and have only a few shillings left.

I meant to write before but I've nothing any good to write about.

I've hit on a bad patch.

Nothing goes right. I don't know how I've continued on at work. Still, when one is running downhill, you have to pull up first before you can face the other way.

Ruth, the handwriting analyst, had been right. Arthur's sadness had soaked through the paper, even in the scant words he'd written on the postcard. Scattered on the hotel bedspread, his letters didn't seem unfamiliar. So too, the watercolors, each highlighting sentimental poetry passages, many of poets like Ernest Dawson and Arthur O'Shaughnessy who had also tragically met early deaths.

The next day, Tom's neighbor Michael drove us all northward to the coast. We passed flint stone and orange brick, triangular-roofed houses, narrow entrances, then suddenly Blickling Hall, one of the great Jacobean houses in East Anglia, like a mirage, far off from the rain-drenched car window. We only had time to stop and look at it from its entrance, a confection of red brick and Ketton limestone, Dutch gables and turrets, the massive yew hedges. We continued to the coastal village of Blakeney, once a port town in medieval times, sitting on the lip of an estuary. That morning, it was cold and rainy, and a bitter wind tore at our flimsy windbreakers, but the hotel was warm, serving hot tea and sandwiches, and a dainty wallpaper, like a child's nursery, lined the walls.

I looked out the row of windows to the flatness of the salt marshes, almost all sky. Blakeney was once an important fishing center with ships making an annual voyage to Iceland. It was also a port with a North Sea trade based on the export of cereals, especially barley and malt, and the import of coal, timber, iron, and roofing tiles. In the early 1800s, they'd tried to construct a new waterway to make it easier for ships to reach the quay. But the port was eventually closed due to bigger ships and continuous silting, and there were no tall sailing ships anymore.

Watching the water, I remembered one of Arthur's watercolors. It was different from the others—he'd only used two colors, blue and black, like a New York skyline, tall buildings against a washed-out sky.

Looking out, I could feel the secrets in the high tides, boats unseen, sunk far out at sea. I could hear the sounds they would make, wood creaking against water, fabric slapping in the wind, and tiny noises of gulls and terns pecking at the sand. Here, in this lonely place, far from everything I'd known, there were also more stories and secrets hidden away.

Europe behind us, David and I landed in Los Angeles on a warm November day. There was no rain here, only the sway of palm trees and a cloudless sky. It reminded me of the luminous light of the South of France and the coastline of Tel Aviv, and I knew the moment we landed that this is where we would stay and make a new home. Three years went by. There was a miscarriage and months of ache for the unborn child, dreams of water, wombs, and blood. Then, pregnant again, the doctor told us this child too might not "stick."

I held on to the word, stick, calling on all its power, to adhere, to fix itself inside of me.

And it did.

Six months later labor started at night, and I hoped for a quick delivery, but I also hoped the baby would be born in the light of day. In my head was a singular thought—that I didn't want its first view of the world to be in darkness. Hearing my wish, Oren was born at ten thirty in the morning. And then the universe heard my other hope, granting it too. It was a wish I told no one, not even David. And when I held him, I breathed a strange sigh of relief. Oren's eyes were ocean blue, the kind that wouldn't change, the kind that had once let some Jewish children pass as gentiles, saving them from slaughter.

Thirty-one

On our last day in Norwich, we took a taxi to Tom's house. Winnie was already there. "Let me make the tea for everyone today," I volunteered, as we sat down in the kitchen, and both Tom and Winnie smiled. While the kettle was boiling, Tom told us more about their "Aunt" Ginny.

"It wasn't until I was in my teens that I learned that Aunt Ginny was not my aunt at all, but actually my maternal grandmother," Tom explained.

"Our mother, Harriet, was the illegitimate daughter of Louisa Jane Reeves, also known as Ginny, but because it had been a disgrace for a woman to have a child out of wedlock, the family hid the family secret and our mother was raised by Louisa's mother, having no contact early on with her own mother," Winnie added.

Talia looked at me as if to ask if we should tell them, and I nodded yes. "Yeah, we know about aunts who aren't really aunts too," Talia said, and I told Tom and Winnie about Rhea.

"It tore our family apart," I said.

"Yes, I know. Secrets can also tear a person apart," Tom suddenly said. "Poor Arthur . . ." He took a breath and started again. "He was misunderstood in our community. He had some friends, but he was different. He sought friendships that were in sympathy with him. It was as though he was in between two worlds. Those were not tolerant times, and men like Arthur had to be careful." Tom paused. "Maybe he found some solace in his correspondence with W. Maybe the little postcard started the whole thing."

Men like Arthur.

Do not disclose.

All the fragile threads came rushing at once in my head—Arthur and Watson, watercolors saved in a fire, Rhea and my father, underlined words.

Arthur had underlined those three words on the postcard, as some kind of code, a way of connecting or reaching out. Tom, too, was telling me all this in code. But I understood. I knew that men like Arthur had had to live in the shadows of widespread prosecutions during the 1940s and 1950s with the threat of aversion and hormone therapies as an alternative to jail time. During WWII gay soldiers were considered mentally unfit. It was not until 1967, four short years after Arthur passed away, that homosexuality in Britain was decriminalized, and not until 2000 that a British soldier could be openly gay.

But I could see Tom didn't want to say any more about it. "I've got some wonderful new biscuits to go with that tea. First cupboard on the right," he said, and Talia got up to get the biscuits. "I've done some of my own digging around about our family, but I still don't know how my mother and father met," Tom said.

"I think I might know," I spoke up.

"How's that?" Tom asked, puzzled.

"When I was looking at the 1901 British census, I came across your father in the district of Tottenham. I think I have a copy here," I said, taking out a folder I'd brought along. "See here." I pointed to the photocopy I'd made of a page of the census from the parish of Saint Peters. "Your mother, Harriet Reeves, fifteen years old, was living with Louisa Reeves at Four Walton Road. Next door to them, at Five Walton, the Maynard family resided, and your father, Arthur Albert Maynard, was their eighteen-year-old son who worked in a furniture shop. Seven years later, your brother, Arthur Thomas, was born in February of 1908, and they were still living on Five Walton Road."

"I never knew that," Tom said.

"Your mother and father were neighbors. That's how they probably met."

"I would never have known that had it not been for you, Leora," Tom said, giving me a fatherly embrace. "I can't even imagine how much research you've done."

"I never knew that either," Winnie said.

"So, you must have done a lot of digging into your own family too. Genealogy and the like? On your father?"

"Sure, a little," I said, stumbling on the words.

Tom looked at me. "That's okay. I understand. Sometimes you have to make a left turn before you get on the road that's right for you."

"Left turn?"

Talia turned to me. "I think he means it's easier to dig into a stranger's story than your own," she said, kissing me on the cheek. "Mom, we actually have to get going. Our train to London is at three thirty," Talia reminded me.

"I guess it's time to go," I said, not wanting to.

I said goodbye to Tom and Winnie, hugging them both and promising to write. At the doorway, Tom suddenly remembered a vivid dream he'd had the night before.

"I was dancing with a group of young girls and wondered if I would be able to keep up with them. Do you think it means something?" Tom asked Talia, his eyes lighting up. "I think it was the jitterbug," he continued.

"Must have been," Talia said.

She was born just hours after David and I attended a performance of the Bolshoi ballet. Nine months plus pregnant, and feeling more whale than human, I hadn't wanted to go, but somehow David had convinced me, and we ended up on one of the top balconies of the Dorothy Chandler Pavilion, the baby kicking and rollicking inside me throughout the entire performance. Twenty-four hours later, Talia was born. I held her for a moment, but then the nurse took her from me and placed her in a tiny oxygen tent near my bed. I was worried and asked the nurse why the tent. "Don't worry. She's just panting a little. She's just like a little dancer," the nurse said.

Thirty-two

That night back in our apartment in London, a hundred thoughts swirled madly as Talia lay sleeping in the next bed. I was done. There was nothing more to do, nothing more to discover. I'd found Arthur, his brother and sister, and I'd returned the postcard to its rightful place. The wild goose chase I'd started a year ago had ended; I'd stumbled on another family's closet of secrets and lies, closed an arc, and even possibly done a good deed. There was nothing more I needed to discover, or was there? Maybe it was time to reroute my GPS from what Tom had called "the left turn."

I'd gone halfway around the world to find the traces of a stranger, but only now, at the end of that journey, had I even thought to decipher the threads of my own family, the connecting dots in my own childhood.

On my return to Los Angeles, jet lag hit hard, but I had a few days to recover before going back to work, and I immediately started on it. Some things I gleaned from history books, others I discovered in scrapbooks, photos, and the documents my father kept in an old metal file cabinet tucked away in a hall closet. I took them home with me, and the old papers and documents still had the smell of my parents' house. Unlike Maynard, though, which consumed me for one year only, my digging into my own family's omissions and secrets started and stopped, often sputtering out completely for years, but always bleeding into my nights.

The early 1990s arrived with a kind of ferocious insistence, a combination of tragedy mixed with redemption. In mid-March of 1992, my best friend from law school was murdered in a terrorist attack on the Israeli embassy in Buenos Aires. And even though Hezbollah took responsibility for the attack, for me, it conjured painful reminders of Argentina's harboring Nazis after WWII. Still, redemption came in the form of my father bringing Theodore Stanescu, the Romanian professor who had saved his life during the Holocaust, to the US to be honored as a "Righteous Gentile," at the Simon Wiesenthal Center. Meeting him, a little man in a threadbare suit, sitting at my parents' dinner table, seemed to me a small sign that the universe could actually right itself.

But in the spring of 1994, a few months after a 6.9 earthquake rocked Los Angeles, cracking walls and swaying our house like a ship at sea, a different kind of earthquake hit.

It was that night, the night that all other hell broke loose.

I hadn't seen Dena in years, but we were in touch by phone. That night she called me, saying she needed my opinion. It was a weekday, and Oren and Talia were already asleep in their rooms, and I was in the bedroom of our first house in North Hollywood.

"It's kind of an ethics question," Dena said, something she'd been wrestling with, a part of some course she was taking, she explained. In the next room, I could hear David turning on the faucets in the bath, and water splashing down noisily into the empty, pinkish tub.

Something about paternity, I half heard her say, and I put up the volume on my phone.

"What if you found out something important, but it might hurt other people? Maybe even shatter their world," she asked. "Would you still tell them?"

I thought for a minute, but the water in the bathroom seemed to get louder and louder. I prattled on for twenty minutes about legalities and practical considerations. "What if someone needed a kidney? Or had a fatal genetic disease?" I posed. "Wouldn't it be right to tell them?"

"I suppose, but . . ." Dena said, and suddenly I felt the weight of her hesitation.

"I think the truth sets you free," I parroted the line from the New Testament, feeling immediately ridiculous, and those words ended our short conversation. I hung up, but the phone stayed in my hand like an unanswered question. In the bathroom, David had shut off the water, and in the silence, it hit me like an unexpected downpour.

"I think I know what she's trying to tell me," I said to David when he came to the bedroom. "I think I understand now." I started to sob. "It all makes sense, right? Everything makes sense now."

I ran out the front door and sat on the stoop. My head was full of water, dammed up with nowhere to go. David followed me minutes later.

"How did I not see it all these years? How could I not have known that Rhea was my father's mistress, and Dena was my half sister? For God's sake, she called my father Aba—Daddy. And Dena's middle name is Bracha. That's my great-grandmother's name. There were so many signs and clues. How could I be so incredibly stupid?"

David put his arms around me, and cradled me. "You were a child. A child accepts what they are told," he tried to console me.

"But I haven't been a child for a long time. I have children of my own. I should have figured it out years ago."

"You have to be ready to figure it out."

Later, I came back into the house, dialed my mother, and told her about my conversation with Dena. An hour later, she called me back and related that she'd confronted my father.

"He admitted it," she said, in a voice I didn't recognize, a voice of finality, a declaration and demarcation that now marked a before and an after, like a death. "After all the times I'd asked him over the years, after all the years of denials, he finally admitted it."

I was angry. I was sad. But mostly, though, I was relieved. The truth had done its job. It had yanked off the layers and years of lies. It too had brought with it a strange redemption. Later that night, I went to the doors of my children's bedrooms and watched them sleep, listening to the sounds of their breathing along with the sound of water in my head, now undammed.

Thirty-three

$\mathcal{So}$ much of the story I didn't know. So much of the story I'd never tried to know.

Buried inside the papers I found in my parents' house, I learned that when I was a year and half, my father was sent from Israel to the US on a cultural exchange singing tour. The letter I found from the government agency that had sent him said the tour was for the purposes of returning to Israel with "cultural information and knowledge." He arrived in the port of New York in August of 1954 with five suitcases on the SS *Jerusalem*, aboard which he apparently also gave several concerts while at sea. His ticket, which he kept, revealed that his address in the US would be c/o a doctor who lived in the small town of Farrell, Pennsylvania. The doctor wasn't a relative, and I'd never heard mention of that town, and when I Googled the address, it came up as an empty lot in a rural area. His documents also showed a change in his birth date from April 22, 1921, to April 21, 1921. I couldn't discern whether it was a simple mistake or intentional.

It seems that for a time he stayed with uncles from my mother's family, traveling to Florida, New York, and Washington, DC, to perform concerts, appear on local Jewish TV stations, and also lead prayers during the High Holy Days. During this time and later on, he used various first and last names—Levi, Lee, Galperin, Galperini, and Halperin. In January of 1955, a Miami Beach newspaper article I

179

discovered reported he'd made his "last appearance in Florida before returning to Israel." But he never did return to live in Israel.

Sometime after he landed in the US, he met Rhea, a first-generation American, who was born Rose in Pennsylvania. A 1930s-era US Census listed her as the daughter of Jacob, a tailor who was born in Russia, and Sophie, also of Russian origin. Later, her mother, Sophie, had leadership roles in the Jewish community, and was one of the founders of the Psychiatric Hospital of Philadelphia and a chapter president of Deborah Hospital, a New Jersey tuberculosis sanitarium, as well as other Jewish welfare organizations. Deeply charitable, Sophie was known for visiting local prisons every Jewish holiday to provide kosher meals for Jewish inmates.

That same census also showed that Rhea had a sister and brother. An earlier census shed light on a first husband, Max, who was born in Russia and whose birth name was Motel. He was the son of a cantor, owned a laundry, and served as president of the Philadelphia Laundry Association.

Six years older than my father, Rhea was divorced from Max with three grown children and had had a full life by the time she'd met my father. A Pan Am flight manifest I found showed she'd flown from Havana, Cuba, to Florida in December 1946, and a ship manifest revealed she'd spent a few weeks in the Canal Zone in the summer of 1948. She'd also been a singer on a Yiddish radio program and had cut several 78 records. And later, despite abuse she'd endured during her first marriage, she took care of her ex-husband, Max, until his dying day.

I never found out exactly how and when my father met Rhea, but I discovered that on April 19, 1955, Rhea had arranged a concert for my father, a "Variety Night" benefit for Deborah Hospital, the same hospital for which her mother was a chapter president. It was seven days before my mother and I arrived from Israel.

Later on, she somehow facilitated a special US Congress Bill dated

July 1956 for the relief of my father authored by Senator Hugh Scott of Pennsylvania. The bill granted my father permanent residence and can still be found in the Congressional record of the 84th Congress, 2nd Session. Who knows how she'd managed that, but she did.

But whatever went on between him and Rhea in those first months in America, it seems that my father wasn't willing to leave my mother, and he sent for her and me. We arrived by plane from Israel in New York City in April of 1955. It was more than strange to find my two-year-old self named as a passenger on the El-Al manifest for that date.

Despite our arrival in the US, it seems that my father and Rhea continued their affair. My half sister, Dena, was born eleven months later, in March of 1956. In July 1955, Rhea covered up the pregnancy by marrying Sol, a Philadelphia clothing manufacturer more than thirty years her senior who, records showed, had been widowed less than five months earlier. Their marriage license described Rhea's occupation as a "divorced fashion consultant," and the two took up residence in Sol's mansion on Philadelphia's Main Line, raising Dena there.

Still, even after Dena was born, my father and Rhea continued to travel together. Rhea and Dena accompanied him to Miami for concerts, staying at ritzy hotels like the Roney Plaza and the Fontainebleau. The Roney, designed by the same architect as the Waldorf in New York City, was famous for its guests, which included the Duke and Duchess of Windsor, Orson Welles, and Rita Hayworth. Desi Arnaz often performed there, and radio commentator Walter Winchell did many of his famous worldwide broadcasts from the Roney's Bamboo Room. The luxurious Fontainebleau had a seventeen-thousand-square-foot lobby, a famous "staircase to nowhere," and six acres of opulent gardens designed to replicate the gardens of Versailles. The hotel photographers took photographs of my father and Dena against the breezy, fake palm tree backdrops, the photos contained in little, plastic key-chain viewers with a one-eyed peephole, the tiny one-inch photos much like the tiny secrets they contained.

Although Rhea had been instrumental in arranging a permanent stay for my father back in 1956, there was still the status of my mother and me, and she was part of that too, driving us up to Niagara Falls, Canada, to have our passports stamped exiting and reentering the US on Friday, October 18, 1957. That day, Niagara Falls was cool and cloudy, with an intermittent rain. Just two weeks before, daredevil Claus Kirkoff had successfully swum through the Lower Rapids, trying to gain illegal entry into the US.

Sometime in March of 1958, it appears my father ended the affair. The last letter to my father I found in the file was one Rhea wrote in her own voice, in handwriting from Miami and not in capital letters like the notes she'd written in Dena's name.

You certainly haven't forgotten that black afternoon and then that painful Sunday. I was going so far—trying to give you freedom, running into the unknown, sick at heart and weary of mind, going away just as you wanted me to do, no matter what it would do to me—and but for the grace of God I could have been killed four different times, and it may still happen on the trip back. And you could walk out on your child that you so sadly neglect, and she needs you so much, without even turning around to look at her twice or even kiss her. I felt as though you drove a sharp knife into my heart when you walked out that door, but I stayed up all night because I was sure you would walk back in. But no, your heart is cold, no feeling, no remembrance of the past. I kept thinking at any moment you would call on the phone and tell me you have come, for you too were suffering, and that your love for me was stronger than all else, and you would be with our darling angel and me

but—another twist of the blade in my heart. If only I could
go to sleep and awaken no more—but no—that's only for the
lucky ones. I must live. My eyes are filled and running over.

Sol died only months later in October of 1958. Rhea moved out
of the mansion on the Main Line, and there were rumors about a
sheriff's sale. In a small clipping in a Philadelphia newspaper, dated
in March of 1960, it was reported she was arrested for passing bad
checks at a car dealership in Philadelphia, and although she made
restitution, she was remanded to Montgomery County Prison to
await extradition proceedings on a pending Dade County Florida
fugitive warrant for not paying her hotel bills in May of 1959.

But despite the letter, the breakup Rhea wrote about, and her
financial problems, she continued to be an important and integral
part of our everyday lives for years, through the 1960s, 1970s, and
1980s, even forming an especially intimate relationship with my
grandparents, my father's parents, who arrived from Israel in May
of 1958, also on the SS *Jerusalem*, and who had supposedly come to
America to "save my parents' marriage."

My grandparents probably knew of the affair and the existence of
baby Dena before they arrived in the US. In letters from my grandparents to my father, they asked about the little *piatra*, the word for
jewel in Romanian. And although they lobbied my father not to
divorce my mother, it seems that they did little to discourage him
from keeping Rhea close.

When my grandmother suffered a heart attack, Rhea donned a
nurse's uniform and stayed with her for days by her bedside at the
hospital. And it was Rhea who brought my grandmother little gifts
and kibitzed with her in the kitchen in Yiddish while my grandmother baked her chocolate babka cake.

Dena too stayed an integral part of our family. In addition to calling
my father *Aba*, she called my mother *Aunt Yael*, and often slept over.

In a September 1959 article from the *Upper Darby News* about my father, who had just started his second year as a cantor for a suburban Philadelphia synagogue, there was a cozy family photograph of him showing a Hebrew scroll to my mother, Dena, and me. Dena, standing closest to my father, was described in the photo caption as a "friend," and in the summer of 1964, my father and my mother took Dena and me to the New York World's Fair, our strange quartet memorialized in a smiling photo of us in front of the iconic "Unisphere."

Also a newcomer to America, with English barely under her belt, my mother buried all her mounting doubts and suspicions and flung herself into her studies at the Philadelphia Academy of Vocal Arts, to which she received a full scholarship immediately following her first audition. Costumed in gorgeous gowns and playing Norina in *Don Pasquale* and Madame Herz in *The Impresario* in the annual Academy concerts, my mother found her little space of joy, love, admiration, and the respect she so achingly yearned for. In May of 1957, she even appeared on local television.

At one point, she summoned up the courage to threaten my father with leaving him and taking me back to Israel with her. But, she'd confided to me, he took away her Israeli passport, and when she turned to the Israeli consulate and asked that they issue her a new one, the 1950s-era paternalistic bureaucracy wouldn't issue her another without her "husband's permission." Dejected, her options were slim. Her mother was still living in a dreary, first-floor, two-room apartment in Tel Aviv, and her younger sister was trying to establish a career in Israel and Europe as a pop singer. There was nowhere to go, and she decided to stay in a marriage where her husband persisted for years in telling her that the affair with Rhea had been "all in her head."

The scrapbooks filled with my parents' glamorous public relations headshots spun a story of a handsome, multitalented, and devoted couple, and in many ways they were. They sang as a duo in local concerts and recitals, music being part of their livelihood and part of the glue that somehow kept them together. They supported one another through lean times, and moves to St. Louis and Los Angeles. They traveled to Europe and South America, and took a mutual pride in their homes and children.

There was still the "why" of it, though, that I couldn't crack open. Why did it happen? And why did my father keep Rhea close? Was it her "can-do" moxie, the way she knew how to get things done, helping my green, immigrant father navigate the waters of his new American home? Was it her desperate and unconditional love for him? And he? Was it love, loneliness, gratitude, or the fact that she had put him on a pedestal, something my mother never did? But something drew him to her that was more than the expensive gifts of clothing and engraved jewelry she lavished on him, and her knowledge about the way things worked in America.

It must have been intoxicating yet familiar for someone like my father, who'd survived the tragedies and deprivation of the war years and the difficult time leading up to Israel's War of Independence, but who longed for the privileged childhood he'd had before the war and the Holocaust.

And then there was the Holocaust. PTSD had only recently been identified as a syndrome that scarred those who had experienced war, extreme violence, and humiliation, many times manifesting in emotional void and detachment, along with survivor's guilt and shame. Why didn't he ever tell me he'd applied to the United Restitution Organization (URO) that facilitated compensation for Holocaust survivors for slave and forced labor performed during the Nazi regime for which he received a token sum? How did I not know he'd approached the International Commission on Holocaust Era Insurance Claims and was denied compensation for the family home destroyed by the Nazis? Did all this play a part in my father's silences and inability to express his feelings?

I thought about his office, full of plaques, diplomas, and awards. Was it just a symptom of his narcissism, or was it, for him, a symbol, written proof that he had overcome the past, made a life, in the aftermath of all those who had not? And hadn't that legacy been passed down to me in my longing, even as a child, to leave something behind as well?

I still had many unanswered questions about my father and Rhea when I finally put my research to bed. I'd wanted clear-cut explanations, but I could only speculate as to why the affair began, why it continued, and why it had morphed over the years into some strange family concoction.

In the end, maybe the hardest thing I discovered was not a fact in a newspaper article, a census, or the papers and photos left behind, but something I'd been a part of, but only half understood, all along. As a child, I loved hearing my parents sing the duet from Mozart's *Don Giovanni*, "Là ci darem la mano." The duet was so beautiful, so silky, and when my father sang it, he seemed to look at my mother with adoring eyes. Their voices were so glorious together, so matched.

Give me your hand, my fairest. Whisper a gentle yes. Come, if for me you carest.

I must have heard them sing it dozens of times, not knowing the meaning of the words in Italian or the plot of the opera. It was only much later that I learned that despite its beautiful melody, the famous duet where Don Giovanni sings to his secret lover was not about love but about deceit. And more than anything I learned from my searching, digging, and excavating into the past, it was this that broke my heart.

Thirty-four

More than ten years went by. It was a decade of milestones—Talia's college graduation, marriages for both Oren and Talia, court closures and my early retirement, a career change for David, and caring for my aging parents. My octogenarian email friend, Bert from Australia, took me up on my casual invitation to visit Los Angeles and stayed with us for two weeks. Kay from the Clinton Avenue apartment in Brooklyn flew in from New York for a long weekend as well. I kept in touch with Tom and Winnie for a few years, exchanging Christmas cards and letters, and visited Tom two more times with David, once in Norwich, another time in Stevenage, where Winnie's daughter resided. But slowly the letters and cards dwindled, and a few years ago, Winnie's daughter wrote me that Tom had passed away. I'd tried to reach out to his family, but I never heard back, and the story of my yearlong search for Arthur Maynard and my friendship with Tom and Winnie melted away, merely an interesting anecdote I sometimes related to new acquaintances.

Then my mother passed away in April 2015 after a rare neurological illness that left her unable to walk, and toward the end, even unable to speak. Her beautiful voice, which always had the clarity of her coloratura soprano, was reduced to a sad slur. It had been so hard to watch my strong mother whittled down to a shell, and for weeks, I wandered around the house, broken and emptied. But I found it hard to cry. One night after the funeral, in the middle of my midnight wanderings, the word *Niagara* and the memory of the photograph and the file came back to haunt me.

It took me a week to remember where I'd stashed the file and the original photograph. I'd buried them somewhere at the bottom of a closet in my office, and its digital version on my newer computer had also somehow disappeared. I finally found the photo and its digital sister, along with the journals I'd written while I'd searched for Arthur Maynard, and Arthur's letters to Tom. I looked at the photo once again and felt it, the little girl who loved both her mother and her Aunt Ree, wedged in between them, ignorant of the chaos around her.

The photo sat on my desk for days until one morning, I decided to look up the origin of the word *Niagara*. The word came from the Iroquoian language meaning a strait *between* two bodies of water, Lake Ontario and Lake Erie. I knew then that there was one more thing I needed to do.

I would have to return to Niagara, to that bridge in the photograph.

But first, I had to refigure where the bridge had stood, and whether it even existed anymore. Niagara had many bridges, and I'd tried and failed, years before, to identify it. Then I found a recent article about an extensive renovation of the William Rankine Generating Station Bridge, built in 1905, and the utility bridge behind it on the Niagara Parkway. The small photo looked promising. I downloaded the photo of the renovation, zooming in and out, comparing it to the bridge in my photo, and it seemed enough of a match for me.

"Look at this." I showed both photos to David.

"Looks like you do have to go," he said, after I pointed out the similarities to him.

"But really? Again? Another crazy trip?"

"Not crazy." He smiled. "It's just a trip."

With David's blessing, the pilgrimage to Niagara now seemed inevitable. Even my impractical plan of tacking it on to a visit with my childhood friend Ivy, who lived in Providence, Rhode Island, which was a long drive from Niagara, seemed preordained too.

I went back online and bought airline tickets for David and me to Boston for early fall 2015. Only weeks later did I realize that the timing would land me in Niagara in October, the same month the photo was taken, fifty-eight years later, and that my plan for a one-day trip there would echo the same one day I'd spent in Niagara with my father, mother, and Rhea in 1957.

When October rolled around, I packed the photo and the "Rhea" file and took them along with me, but before I left, I did one more thing. I finally sent Dena photocopies of the contents of the file. For years I'd wrestled with it, worrying it would be too painful for her to read. But just as she had done that one night, when she told me so many years ago the truth of our childhood, I knew I couldn't keep it from her any longer.

On the plane to Boston, I was happy I'd also planned to spend a few days with Ivy. We'd had so many seminal moments together, sleeping with our SAT books under our pillows, half-laughingly convinced it would help us score well the following day, and rehashing comical wish-we-hadn't-done-that stories when we were freshman students in Jerusalem together. It turned out to be a good segue—Ivy's two-story house on a tree-lined street reminded me of Tom's cottage in Norwich, as well as her kitchen full of the smells of her cinnamon biscotti and scones. Diane, another close childhood friend, drove up from Philadelphia, and the three of us went apple picking together in Connecticut, and explored the town of Northampton, the Berkshires afire with the red and gold of October foliage. It felt good to be part of a different kind of threesome, friends who had known me as a child, friends who had known my parents, sending me off to close the final chapter.

"You know, that's one really crazy photo," Ivy said, as David and I were about to leave three days later. "And the fact that your father took a photo of your mother and her, and you in between."

"Yeah. Me, in between. Crazy," I echoed.

"Good luck," Ivy yelled out as we backed out of her driveway. "Take the first left, then head up straight to the highway," she said.

"Yes, first a left, then straight ahead." I laughed, thinking of Tom.

David did all the driving, following Interstate 90 almost all the way, except when Waze told us otherwise. We only stopped once for gas and coffee, and made it to the Canadian border in about seven hours, almost the same amount of driving time it would have been for my parents, Rhea, and me from Philadelphia back in 1957.

People had warned us about the city of Niagara itself, and driving into the Canadian side of the falls, it proved to be exactly what we'd expected. There were high-rise hotels all around the falls, kitschy, honky-tonk casinos and an IMAX, duty-free shops and a tacky Ripley's Believe It or Not Museum. We arrived just as night fell, and although our hotel boasted a view of the Horseshoe Falls, the room also looked out at the jumbo LED screen stapled to the facade of a casino, the screen blinking advertising twenty-four hours a day.

In the lobby, I scanned the rows of "Niagara Attractions" brochures near the concierge's desk. They were full of color photographs of the falls, the ads in Day-Glo, and they didn't mesh with the black-and-white image of the photograph that was lodged inside me or the October sky of the photo, colored only in smudges of gray.

It was too late to do anything but eat dinner, take a quick walk on the deserted, windy streets, then bed. But I couldn't sleep, and knowing that I'd only allotted enough time to see the falls and find the bridge, I dug out my iPad from my suitcase and watched a video tour of Table Rock, at the foot of the Horseshoe Falls.

There was only a half-empty maze of gates near the ticket window, not much of a line at the entrance. Tourists were directed toward a couple of elevators and were given disposable ponchos. Then a guide briefed the group on the history of the falls as they descended 125 feet down. Built in 1889, a tunnel was excavated through the rock to an exit well behind the falls, the guide explained. Down below would be a network of 150 feet of tunnel burrowed behind the great sheet of Niagara Falls. When the tunnels were first built, only lanterns illuminated the cave-like corridors of rock.

When the tour group stepped out of the virtual elevator, there was no mistaking the roar of the water, its vibration booming in my chest. Walking away from the shaft, the virtual tour I was watching followed the path of the tunnel, all white, thick, electric conduit and light fixtures running across one side. The path led to two arched pools of rushing water and the observation decks. And there was the edge of the falls, just about twenty-five feet above the river level.

The scene was almost blinding. All I could see was a whiteout of water. Then, down the stairs to the open observatory. Six steps down from the tunnel entrance. The passageway looked like a bomb shelter carved into the rock. Two other staircases led up to the covered, upper observation deck. The railings were painted aqua green, odd against the concrete and rock, both stained and worn out from the years of relentless water. The lower deck ended in a half circle, its floor wet and slippery. I could see the pallid water, the sea of transparent, yellow hooded rain ponchos billowing like cellophane in the sprays created by the force of the falls. Near the edge, people posed, wet and translucent by the railing, smiling against the bluster, and I could almost feel the spray of the falls.

In the morning, David and I walked from the hotel down to the two-thousand-foot-wide Horseshoe Falls. It was "dead season," the Starbucks barista had told David, and there were very few tourists.

From afar, I could see a solitary boat, the *Maid of the Mist*, and the passengers who all wore blue rain gear, packed together, and the boat looked like a box of cobalt beads. I watched it as it pressed forward toward the falls.

We walked past ancient optical viewers and the snow-white, green-eyed birds that sat unafraid on the wrought iron fence.

"If you focus on one spot on the water, you feel like you're going to be swept away," someone said, behind me, the mist as thick as smoke.

I heard the sound of it—the water dropping into the gorge, the thirteen stories of water, and I could almost feel myself falling, submerged beneath the trillion of gallons of waters being forced through.

I stepped back from the spray and the mist, Niagara's rush of water.

We were about to go turn back to the hotel and get into the car to look for the bridge when I got a call from Talia.

"I was at your house, looking for something I'd left near your computer, and found something," she said, excited. "I just had to call you."

"Found what?" I put the phone on speaker.

"It was in the pile on your desk, kind of stuck behind."

"What was?" I'd been clearing up some of my old paperwork and had stacked my original Maynard journals, research, and Arthur's letters to Tom on my desk to be refiled and stored away after my trip.

"Listen to this. You even underlined it. Arthur wrote that he would come to visit Tom in Canada one day *to see the lovely north woods during an Indian summer . . . to visit such places with names musical-sounding . . . like your own Ontario, and Niagara.*" Niagara, Mom. And you're there, so weird, right?' she said. "I couldn't believe it. I just had to call you. Mom, maybe you're in Niagara for Arthur too?"

As bizarre as that sounded, part of me wanted to believe it. Maybe my mother's firm belief in meant-to-be had been passed down through me to my daughter. "I remember reading about Arthur's plan to join Tom in Canada. But Tom had told me Arthur could never save enough money to make the trip," I said.

"Call me after you find the bridge," Talia said.

"Here for Arthur too?" David repeated. "I guess that wouldn't surprise me at this point," he said, laughing. "But you know what?"

he added, looking past the falls. "I don't think we have to get into our car and drive to find the bridge. I have a strange feeling it's just around this path, in walking distance." We started toward the back of the falls.

Soon, I started to sense that he was right. Just steps away from the back of the Horseshoe Falls, I saw it. There were no tourists here, not much for sightseers to view, only a lone groundskeeper seated on a large mower, going back and forth on a small patch of lawn. The bridge was over the start of the catch basin, which made the water seem tamer here. As we walked, the sky became cloudier, everything turning gray, and only the grass seemed to stay green.

I ran a couple of steps ahead. "This is it. It's the bridge," I called back to David. "I know it. We found it."

I stood still for a few minutes and waited for some epiphany I was sure would come, but it didn't. Not one memory of the trip to Niagara, the falls or the bridge, my parents or Rhea. There was nothing I remembered besides the image that had been captured in the photograph, but somehow it didn't matter.

The renovation had made the utility ice bridge into a pedestrian walkway, and tall buildings and the Skylon Tower were now in the background. But still the bridge echoed the one in my old photo.

I'd brought the photo with me, along with the contents of the Rhea file, folded up. I took the photo out of my handbag. I remembered seeing some "looking into the past" photos on the internet, and I held up the old, square photo, positioning it and overlapping it to meet the horizontal lines of the current view of the bridge.

David helped me climb up on the stone edge of the bridge. It was higher than I'd thought, and I could hear my mother.

I was afraid. I was afraid you would fall.

Sitting there, I could feel the forces of gravity pulling me down now, the sky drawing and tugging at me, hear the water rushing, and for a moment I too thought I might slip off, just as my mother had feared so many years ago.

But I also heard my mother's silver voice. She was Rusalka again the invisible lake nymph yearning to be mortal in the otherworldly place of wood sprites and water gnomes. The nymph's formless body embraced her faithless prince with the one movement she could marshal—a wave of water. And although the witch warned Rusalka that she would lose her voice, the water nymph battled against the charms of the foreign princess who was her rival for the prince's affection. And Rusalka chose muteness to be with her prince.

I looked out. It was David across from me now. David who had driven the entire way from Providence to Niagara Falls without a word of complaint or question of the path I'd embarked on ten years ago—the postcard, the year of research, the trips to London and Norwich, the monies spent. I was grateful for his love and his willingness to say yes.

He took more photos, then helped me down from my perch on the bridge. It was in his arms that I felt it, the arc completed, a circle returned to its starting point. He showed me the photo he'd taken of me on his phone. I was on that bridge, just myself, separate, and no longer in between.

We walked back to the edge of the falls. We would have to hurry to start our seven-hour trip back to Providence and get there before dark, but I stopped again.

I closed my eyes. It was time to banish them, one by one, every secret.

And it was time to throw away the file.

I chucked it in the nearest trash bin.

And with it, I sent them all away, the hurts and betrayals, for my mother and father, for Rhea and my sister, for my brother, for Arthur, and then for me. I cast them out for my children too, and for their children to come. I sent their secrets over the roar of the falls and hurled them down into the gorge of water. And then I looked back at the bridge one more time, and even though it was day, and the streetlamps were still unlit, I was sure I saw it. It was there, or maybe not—just a tiny flicker of light at the top of the lamppost.

Acknowledgments

This memoir was not easy to write. It took years, new perspectives, and a lot of soul searching.

I am also indebted to many people for helping with its birth.

First, I'm delighted to thank my publisher, Brooke Warner, who has given voice to so many women and their stories, something deeply appreciated by me, someone who, as a young reader, yearned for more books written by women.

Thanks too to all the diligent and nurturing people at She Writes Press, Lauren Wise and Samantha Strom, project managers and masters of the complicated processes of birthing a book into the world. Many thanks also to my great PR team at Sparkpoint Studio, Crystal Patriarche, Madison Ostrander and Tabitha Bailey.

Family. My dear parents, Yael and Levi, are no longer with us, but the threads of their lives, their lessons to strive for accomplishment and relevancy, and their love remain within me. My brother, Ron, my sister, Dena, my son, Oren, my brother-in-law, Zach, my son-in-law, Israel, my sisters-in-law, Karen and Irit, my mother-in-law, Edith, my brother-in-law, Ralph, and my daughter-in-law, Lin, have all been there to support and encourage me.

My husband, David, a special spirit from the moment I met him, never wavers in telling me to trust myself. I could not do what I do without him.

Friends. There are so many—Ivy and Diane, who have known me

since elementary school, Bob and Agatha, Linda, Jackie, and Carolyn, who slogged through drafts of this memoir with caring suggestions, and so many others.

Most of all, I'm so grateful to my daughter, Talia, who came along with me on this journey. Whenever I straggled, she gave me a push. Whenever I faltered, she told me it would be okay. Whenever I pouted and doubted, she made me laugh, then and now.

Thank you, each and every one of you.

About the Author

Leora Krygier is a former Los Angeles Superior Court, Juvenile Division judge. She's the author of *When She Sleeps* (Toby Press),which was lauded for its "luminous prose" (Newsweek) and praised by *Booklist, Library Journal,* and *Kirkus.* It was also a New York Public Library Selection for "Best Books for the Teen Age." She's also the author of *Juvenile Court: A Judges Guide for Young Adults and their Parents* (Rowan & Littlefield) and *Keep Her* (She Writes Press), a young adult novel reviewed as a "vibrantly dazzling literary cocktail on the restorative powers of love." She lives in Los Angeles with her husband, David.

SELECTED TITLES FROM SHE WRITES PRESS

She Writes Press is an independent publishing company founded to serve women writers everywhere. Visit us at www.shewritespress.com.

Surviving the Survivors: A Memoir by Ruth Klein $16.95, 978-1-63152-471-4
With both humor and deep feeling, Klein shares the story of her parents—who survived the Holocaust but could not overcome the tragedy they had experienced—and their children, who became indirect victims of the atrocities endured by the generation before them.

Jumping Over Shadows: A Memoir by Annette Gendler
$16.95, 978-1-63152-170-6
Like her great-aunt Resi, Annette Gendler, a German, fell in love with a Jewish man—but unlike her aunt, whose marriage was destroyed by "the Nazi times," Gendler found a way to make her impossible love survive.

The Beauty of What Remains: Family Lost, Family Found by Susan Johnson Hadler $16.95, 978-1-63152-007-5
Susan Johnson Hadler goes on a quest to find out who the missing people in her family were—and what happened to them—and succeeds in reuniting a family shattered for four generations.

The Butterfly Groove: A Mother's Mystery, A Daughter's Journey by Jessica Barraco $16.95, 978-1-63152-800-2
In an attempt to solve the mystery of her deceased mother's life, Jessica Barraco retraces the older woman's steps nearly forty years earlier—and finds herself along the way.

Implosion: Memoir of an Architect's Daughter by Elizabeth W. Garber
$16.95, 978-1-63152-351-9
When Elizabeth Garber, her architect father, and the rest of their family move into Woodie's modern masterpiece, a glass house, in 1966, they have no idea that over the next few years their family's life will be shattered—both by Woodie's madness and the turbulent 1970s.

Don't Call Me Mother: A Daughter's Journey from Abandonment to Forgiveness by Linda Joy Myers $16.95, 978-1-938314-02 -5
Linda Joy Myers's story of how she transcended the prisons of her childhood by seeking—and offering—forgiveness for her family's sins.